One Lap Around California

Don W. Lake

Orofino Press

Orofino, Idaho

ISBN 978-1480025622

Sources

Material for "One Lap Around California was primarily gathered (except otherwise noted) from unrestricted internet sites. Which material to include, and which to exclude, were chosen by the editor's whim, based entirely on what interested him.

One Lap Around California

Compiled and Edited by Don W. Lake

This book is dedicated to my wife Pat. Without her love, understanding, support, and incredible patience none of this would have been possible.

Forward

It's a simple idea. Drive all the way around California, keeping as close to the border as possible without ever crossing it, yet staying on excellent roads: California highways, U.S. Highways, or even Interstate Highways.

Each person's experience will, of course, be different, but each one will be highlighted by:
- Bests – such as the beach named the best in America or the Navy base named the best in the world
- Birthplaces – such as the birthplace of the physical fitness boom of the 20th Century
- Busiest – the world's busiest port of entry
- Firsts – such as the first tunnel under an airport runway, the first motel in the world, or the US Olympic training center designed from the ground up to be an Olympic training center
- Highest – the highest point in the continental United States
- Hottest – the hottest place in the United States
- Largest – such as the largest alpine lake in North the world's largest resort hotel (when it opened), the largest Japanese Segregation Center, the largest man made small boat harbor, the largest concentration of lava tube caves, or the largest wood lath building in the world (when it opened).
- Last – such as the last non-Essex class aircraft carrier from WWII, or the last working lumber style cookhouse
- Longest Running – "major" street race in North America
- Most – such as the most photographed bridge in the world, the most beautiful government building in America the most grand Victorian house in America, the Southernmost Russian settlement in North America, or the most visited American Castle
- Oldest – such as the oldest tree in the world, California's oldest working wharf, or the oldest human remains in North America

- Only – mobile national monument
- Rarest – species of pine tree in the United States
- Smallest – such as the smallest county, by population in California or the smallest place ever to host the Olympic Games
- Tallest – such as the tallest trees in the world, or the tallest thermometer in the world

    The list of those things included here is not meant to be comprehensive, just representative of all of the amazing, unique and otherwise noteworthy within California's borders. They are not, like Burma Shave Signs, always visible from the road. Some are. Some are even part of the road itself. Others are nearby and need a short drive to be visited. All are included because the editor thought them interesting.

California

Table of Contents

Section 1: Border to Dana Point

Section 2: Dana Point to Long Beach

Section 3: Los Angeles County

Section 4: Oxnard to Santa Cruz

Section 5: Half Moon Bay to Eureka

Section 6: Eureka to South Lake Tahoe

Section 7: Markleeville to San Yasidro

Section 1

Border to California1 in Dana Point

Interstate 5 – to California75 – to Interstate 5
84 miles

San Ysidro Border Crossing

Less than 20 miles south of downtown San Diego lies the world's busiest port of entry -
the international border crossing between San Ysidro, and Tijuana, Mexico.

San Ysidro is home to the world's busiest land border crossing, where U.S. Interstate 5 crosses into Mexico at Tijuana. In the 2005 U.S. fiscal year, more than 17 million vehicles and 50 million people entered the United States at the San Ysidro Port of Entry. The great majority of these are workers (both of Mexican and U.S. nationality) commuting from Tijuana to jobs in the greater San Diego area and throughout Southern California

There is also reverse traffic, both of workers traveling to maquiladoras in Mexico and those purchasing services or seeking entertainment in Tijuana. Crossing times are often slow at San Ysidro, particularly for those entering the United States in cars. For this reason many cross on foot, the line for which is frequently much faster than the vehicle line. Some foot travelers own a car in each country, and keep them in one of the large parking lots located near the border post, or use the respective public transportation systems of both cities (both systems have a bus station built solely to serve the border crossing point, and the San Diego Trolley runs from downtown San Diego to the border crossing).

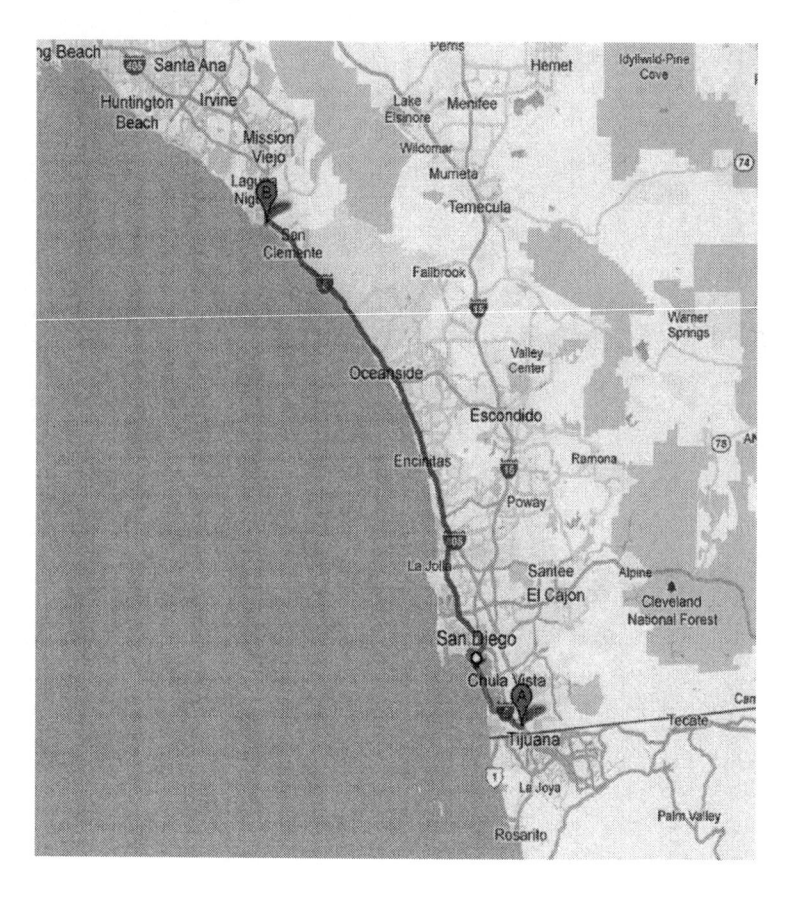

Border to Dana Point (Google Maps)

San Ysidro Border Crossing

     Trucks are generally instructed to use the border crossing in Otay Mesa instead of the San Ysidro one.

     A proposed expansion of the San Ysidro Port of Entry is taking place in three parts and is scheduled to be completed in the spring of 2014. The $577 million project will expand and veer Interstate 5 to the west. Slated to be built are a new northbound inspection facility, including primary vehicle inspection booths, a secondary inspection area, an administration space, and a pedestrian-processing facility. A new southbound inspection facility is also planned.

San Diego Trolley

The Tijuana River Estuary, and Border Field State Park

At the southwestern most corner of the United States lies a mystical land, a magical place of secret native lore, gently flowing seasonal streams, a great and wide river, and vast, verdant parklands eagerly waiting discovery by flocks of travelers, tourists, and naturalists.

These hidden lands are called the Tijuana River Estuary and California Border Field State Park. While separate and apart as political entities they share the same cool and gentle expanse of flowing waters and interesting, even rare, native flora and fauna.

International Border at Border Field State Park

The view here in this hidden place is of miles of verdant, moist, and shaded river bottom, and then finally a wide alluvial plume which releases these waters to the sea. Here, they mix with the great Pacific Ocean and that ocean's powerful currents swirl these rich waters northward along the California coast for as much as 50 miles.

Imperial Beach

Imperial Beach is the most southwesterly city, and southwesterly residence, in the continental United States. The city occupies the extreme southwest corner of the continental United States: bordered by Tijuana, Mexico to the south, Coronado, to the north, the San Diego Bay to the east and the Pacific Ocean to the west.

Imperial Beach is located in San Diego County, the fifth most-populous county in the United States and part of the San Diego Metropolitan Area, the 17th largest metropolitan area in the United States with over 3 million people. It is also part of the San Diego – Tijuana metropolitan area, the largest bi-national metropolitan area shared between the United States and Mexico with over 5 million people. Despite the large population surrounding the city, Imperial Beach maintains a small residential feel.

Founded in June 1887, the city takes its name from Imperial County, a desert climate 100 miles east. Farmers and land owners from the Imperial Valley came to the area in the late 1880s seeking cooler weather during summer months. In March 1887, over 2,000 laborers descended upon nearby Coronado, to construct the Hotel del Coronado, the largest resort in the world at the time. A large amount of the workers stayed in Imperial Beach and some would later make it their permanent homestead.

Imperial Beach Pier

Imperial Beach encompasses nearly 4 miles of beach including a dog friendly area and employs a year round lifeguard staff. Beach volleyball, surfing and body boarding are popular in Imperial Beach with activities concentrated north and south of the Imperial Beach Pier and the Boca Rio beach break, one of San Diego County's best surf spots. The area around Imperial Beach Pier known as Pier Plaza showcases plaques placed on surfboard benches that tell the story of how the city's big waves had an impact on surfing from 1937 to the 1950s. Nearby Border Field State Park signifies the most southern beach on the west coast and allows beachgoers in the United States to correspond verbally with beachgoers in Mexico. The city connects to nearby Coronado, named Best Beach in America in May 2012, by way of the Silver Strand, a narrow, 7 mile long isthmus.

Silver Strand State Beach

Silver Strand State Beach features extensive beaches on both the Pacific Ocean and San Diego Bay. Combined with the area's mild climate, the beaches make Silver Strand one of the area's finest recreation destinations. Camping, swimming, surfing, boating, water-skiing, volleyball, and picnicking are popular activities. Anglers can fish for perch, corbina, grunion and yellow-fin croaker.

Silver Strand State Beach

Park facilities include four large parking lots, which can accommodate up to 1,000 vehicles. Restroom and cold showers are available on each side of the park. Beach restrooms are for Day-Use visitors. Per Coastal Commission regulations, campers must be in fully self-contained vehicles. Fire rings for cookouts are available on the beach during summer.

The bay side of the park offers views of San Diego Bay. Three pedestrian tunnels lead from the parking lots under the highway to the bay side of the park. (The bay side of the park is restricted to pedestrian traffic only. No vehicles are allowed in the tunnels or on the bay side.) The water in the bay area is usually warmer and calmer, perfect for swimming and sailing. Ramadas, tables, barbecue pits, and fire rings are available in the area. South of the developed area, there are one and a half miles of ocean and natural preserve. Strolling along the beach, visitors may see moon snail shells, cockle shells, and an occasional sand dollar in the sand.

Hotel del Coronado

Hotel del Coronado (also known as The Del and Hotel del) is a beachfront luxury hotel in the city of Coronado, just across the San Diego Bay from San Diego. It is one of the few surviving examples of an American architectural genre: the wooden Victorian beach resort. It is one of the oldest and largest all-wooden buildings in California and was designated a National Historic Landmark in 1977, and is a designated California Historical Landmark. When it opened in 1888, it was the largest resort hotel in the world. It has hosted presidents, royalty, and celebrities through the years.

Hotel del Coronado

***Coronado*Error! Bookmark not defined. Bay Bridge**
     This award-winning bridge quickly became an area landmark after its opening on August 3, 1969. The distinctive curve and soaring sweep of the San Diego-Coronado Bridge was the first structural conquest of San Diego Bay, joining the Island of Coronado and City of San Diego.
The 2.1-mile long bridge interchanges with Interstate 5 in San Diego and becomes Route 75 in Coronado. With a vertical clearance of approximately 200 feet, the tallest ships can pass beneath it. Its distinctive towers and graceful curve brought it the "Most Beautiful Bridge" Award of Merit from the American Institute of Steel Construction in 1970.

Coronado Bay Bridge

    Beginning at the specially designed toll plaza in Coronado, the traffic ascends at a 4.67 percent grade, curving 80 degrees toward San Diego. Clusters of submerged piles support the 30 mission-arch shaped concrete piers. The 54-inch diameter piles were driven and jetted to depths of 100 feet in the Bay's bottom. All of the braces and stiffeners for the bridge are inside the box girder, providing the slender super-structure with a smooth exterior. The 34-inch high barrier railing is safety designed to redirect vehicles back onto the roadway with little or no damage, and low enough to permit an unobstructed view while crossing the bridge. The center lane of the five-lane roadway is reserved as a safety median and a reversible lane to provide three lanes of peak-hour traffic.

Petco Park

Petco Park is an open-air ballpark in downtown San Diego. It opened in 2004, replacing Qualcomm Stadium as the home park of Major League Baseball's San Diego Padres. Before then, the Padres shared Qualcomm Stadium with the National Football League's San Diego Chargers. Petco Park is named after the pet supplies retailer Petco, which is based in San Diego and paid for the naming rights.

Petco Park

The ballpark is located between 7th and 10th avenues, south of J Street. The southern side of the stadium is bounded by San Diego Trolley light rail tracks along the north side of Harbor Drive (which serve the adjacent San Diego Convention Center). The portion of K Street between 7th and 10th is now closed to automobiles and serves as a pedestrian promenade along the back of the left and center field outfield seating (and also provides access to the "Park at the Park" behind center field). Two of the stadium's outfield entrance areas are located at K Street's intersections with 7th and 10th Avenues. The main entrance, behind home plate, is at the south end of Park Boulevard (at Imperial) and faces the San Diego Trolley 12th & Imperial Transit Center.

San Diego Convention Center

The San Diego Convention Center is the primary convention center in San Diego. It is located in the Marina district of downtown San Diego near the Gaslamp Quarter. The convention center offers 615,701 square feet of exhibit space. As of 2009 it was the 24th largest convention facility in North America. It was designed by Canadian architect Arthur Erickson. Capacity for the facility is 125,000.

San Diego Convention Center

The center's most distinguishing feature is the Sails Pavilion, a 90,000-square-foot exhibit and special event area. The Sails Pavilion's roof consists of distinctive Teflon-coated fiberglass "sails" intended to reflect San Diego's maritime history, as well as to advertise the center's proximity to the San Diego shore. The Pavilion was originally built as an open-air facility under the roof. However, the center found it hard to convince potential users to book an open-air facility, so the Pavilion area was enclosed in glass, greatly expanding the usable area of the center.

USS Midway

USS Midway (CVB/CVA/CV-41) was an aircraft carrier of the United States Navy, the lead ship of her class, and the first to be commissioned after the end of World War II. Active in the Vietnam War and in Operation Desert Storm, she is currently a museum ship at the USS Midway Museum, in San Diego.

USS Midway

She is the only remaining US aircraft carrier of the World War II era that is not an *Essex*-class aircraft carrier. When she was completed in 1945, she was the first US warship that was unable to utilize the Panama Canal due to her size.

USS Midway was laid down 27 October 1943 by Newport News Shipbuilding Co., Newport News, Virginia. Her revolutionary hull design was based on what would have been the *Montana*-class battleship and gave her superior maneuverability over all previous carriers. She was launched 20 March 1945; sponsored by Mrs. Bradford William Ripley, Jr.; and commissioned 10 September 1945, Captain Joseph F. Bolger in command.

In August 1991, *USS Midway* departed Yokosuka and returned to Pearl Harbor. Here, she turned over with *Independence* which was replacing *Midway* as the forward-deployed carrier in Yokosuka. *Midway* then sailed to San Diego where she was decommissioned at Naval Air Station North Island on 11 April 1992 in a ceremony in which the main speaker was Secretary of Defense Dick Cheney. She was stricken from the Naval Vessel Register on 17 March 1997. During the decommissioning process, she was used to film portions of the movie *At Sea*, a documentary on carrier life shown only at the Navy Museum in Washington D.C. Both sailors and their families participated in the filming of the homecoming scenes.

On 30 September 2003, *USS Midway* began her journey from the Navy Inactive Ship Maintenance Facility, Bremerton, Washington, to San Diego, in preparation for use as a museum and memorial. She was docked at the Charles P. Howard Terminal in Oakland, during the first week in October while the construction of her pier in San Diego was completed. Then, on 10 January 2004 the ship was moored at her final location at the Broadway Pier in downtown San Diego, where she was opened to the public on 7 June 2004. In the first year of operation, the museum doubled attendance projections by welcoming 879,281 guests aboard.

On April 3, 2012, it was announced that *USS Midway* would be the site of a college basketball game between the Syracuse Orange and the San Diego State Aztecs on November 9, 2012.

San Diego Maritime Museum

The Maritime Museum of San Diego established in 1948, preserves one of the largest collections of historic sea vessels in the United States. Located in the San Diego Bay, the centerpiece of the museum's collection is the *Star of India*, an 1863 iron bark. The museum maintains the MacMullen Library and Research Archives aboard the 1898 ferryboat *Berkeley*. The museum also publishes the quarterly peer-reviewed journal *Mains'l Haul: A Journal of Pacific Maritime History*.

San Diego Maritime Museum

The Maritime Museum is located on the west side of North Harbor Drive, between the ends of Ash Street and Grape Street, south of San Diego International Airport.

Santa Fe Depot

Union Station in San Diego, also known as the Santa Fe Depot, is a train station built by the Atchison, Topeka and Santa Fe Railway to replace the small Victorian-style structure erected in 1887 for the California Southern Railroad Company. The Spanish Colonial Revival style station is listed on the National

Register of Historic Places. Its architecture, particularly the signature twin domes, is often echoed in the design of modern buildings in Downtown San Diego. A wing now houses the downtown branch of the Museum of Contemporary Art San Diego.

    The Santa Fe Depot officially opened on March 8, 1915, to accommodate visitors to the Panama-California Exposition. The depot was completed during a particularly optimistic period in the City's development, and represents the battle waged by the City of San Diego to become the West Coast terminus of the Santa Fe Railway system's transcontinental railroad, a fight that was ultimately lost to the City of Los Angeles.

Santa Fe Depot

In its heyday, the facility not only handled Santa Fe traffic but also that of the San Diego and Arizona Railway (SD&A) and San Diego Electric Railway (SDERy). The designation was officially changed to "San Diego Union Station" in response to the SD&A's completion of its own transcontinental line in December 1919. The Santa Fe resumed solo operation of the station in January, 1951 when the San Diego and Arizona Eastern Railway (successor to the SD&A) discontinued passenger service, the SDERy having ceased operation some two years earlier.

The historic depot is located in Centre City (Downtown San Diego) and is still an active transportation center, providing services to Amtrak, the San Diego Coaster, the San Diego Trolley, and the San Diego Metropolitan Transit System bus system. Of the 73 California stations served by Amtrak, San Diego was the third busiest in FY2010, boarding or detraining an average of nearly 2000 passengers daily. It is Amtrak's eleventh-busiest station nationwide.

Balboa Park

Balboa Park is a 1,200-acre urban cultural park in San Diego. The park is named after the Spanish maritime explorer Vasco Núñez de Balboa. It was the location of the 1915 Panama–California Exposition and 1935 California Pacific International Exposition which each created architectural landmarks for the park.

The park's site was placed in reserve in 1835, making it one of the oldest sites in the United States dedicated to public recreational use. In addition to open space areas, natural vegetation green belts, gardens and walking paths, it contains a variety of cultural attractions including many museums, several theaters, and the world famous San Diego Zoo. There are also many recreational facilities and several gift shops and restaurants.

Balboa Park, and the historic Exposition buildings, were declared a National Historic Landmark and National Historic Landmark District in 1977, and placed on the National Register of Historic Places. Balboa Park is managed and maintained by the stewardship of the Parks and Recreation Department of the City of San Diego.

The park is essentially rectangular in form, bounded by Sixth Avenue to the west, Upas Street to the north, 28th Street to the east, and Russ Boulevard to the south. The rectangle has been modified by the addition of the Marston Hills natural area in the northwest corner of the park, while the southwest corner of the rectangle is occupied by a portion of the Cortez Hill neighborhood of Downtown San Diego and San Diego High School[1], both of which are separated from the park by Interstate 5. Also encroaching on the northern perimeter of the park is Roosevelt Middle School.

Two north-south canyons – Cabrillo Canyon and Florida Canyon – traverse the park, and separate it into three distinct mesas. The Sixth Avenue Mesa is a narrow strip bordering Sixth Avenue on the western edge of the park, which provides areas of passive recreation, grassy spaces, and tree groves. The Central Mesa is home to much of the park's cultural facilities, and includes scout camps, the San Diego Zoo, the Prado, and Inspiration Point. East Mesa is home to Morley Field and many of the active recreation facilities in the park.

---

[1] Editor's Note: The editor's oldest daughter teaches at San Diego High School. She gets to experience the park every school day.

Balboa Park

In 1948, California State Route 163 was constructed to run through Cabrillo Canyon and pass under the Cabrillo Bridge. This stretch of road, initially named the Cabrillo Freeway, has been called one of America most beautiful parkways. A portion of Interstate 5 was constructed through the park in the 1950s. In total, freeways take up 111 acres of land that had been initially designated for the park.

Surrounding the park are many of San Diego's older neighborhoods, including Downtown, Bankers Hill, North Park, and Golden Hill.

The entire Balboa Park is a primary attraction in San Diego and the region. The park's landscape has many mature, and sometimes rare, trees and groves creating an urban forest for San Diego. Many of the original trees were planted by the renowned American landscape designer, botanist, plantswoman, and gardener Kate Sessions. She was a forerunner of using drought tolerant and California native plants in garden design, establishing a nursery to propagate and grow for the park and the public.

Balboa Park

Throughout the park there are a number of gardens including: Alcazar Garden, Botanical Building, Desert Cactus Garden, Casa del Rey Moro Garden, Inez Grant Parker Memorial Rose Garden, Japanese Friendship Garden, Bird Park, George W. Marston House and Gardens, Palm Canyon and Zoro Garden

El Prado is a long, wide, promenade and boulevard running through the center of the park. Most of the buildings lining this street are in the Spanish Colonial Revival architecture style, a richly ornamented eclectic mixture of European Spanish architecture and the Spanish Colonial architecture of New Spain-Mexico. Along this boulevard are many of the park's museums and cultural attractions, including the San Diego Museum of Man, the San Diego Museum of Art, the Museum of Photographic Arts, the San Diego Art Institute, the San Diego Model Railroad Museum, the San Diego Natural History Museum, the San Diego History Center, the Reuben H. Fleet Science Center, and the Timken Museum of Art. Other features along El Prado include the Reflection Pond, the latticed Botanical Building, and the Bea Evenson Fountain, Adjacent to the promenade is the San Diego Air & Space Museum

Cabrillo Bridge, Balboa Park

   Theatrical and musical venues include the Spreckels Organ Pavilion featuring one of the world's largest outdoor pipe organs; the Old Globe Theatre complex, which includes a replica of Shakespeare's Globe Theatre as well as an outdoor stage and a Theatre in the round; and the Starlight Bowl – an outdoor amphitheatre. The Casa Del Prado Theater is the home of San Diego Junior Theatre, the country's oldest children's theatre program. The House of Pacific Relations International Cottages collected on El Prado offer free entertainment shows.

The Botanical Building, a very large lath house, was built in 1915 from a design by Carleton Winslow. Botanical Building was the largest wood lath structure in the world when it was built in 1915 for the Panama-California Exposition. The lath house features large specimen palms and other plants inside and is located next to a long reflecting pool on the El Prado side.

Cactus Garden, Balboa Park

Located in the eastern third of the park is the Morley Field Sports Complex. Included in this complex are: the Balboa Park Golf Complex, which contains a public 18-hole golf course and 9-hole executive course; the San Diego Velodrome; baseball and softball fields; the USTA-honored Balboa Tennis Club and tennis courts; archery ranges; the Bud Kearn public swimming pool; and a disc golf course.

Among the institutions and facilities within the park's borders but not administered by the city's Parks Department are the San Diego Zoo, the Naval Medical Center San Diego (NMCSD), and San Diego High School. Other attractions in various areas of the park include chess and bridge outdoor tables, horseshoe pits, playgrounds, walking and jogging trails, sports fields and courts, and picnic areas. Clubs and facilities for petanque and lawn bowling are based in the park.

Reflecting Pool, Balboa Park

Spain and later Mexico made a practice of setting aside large tracts of land for the common use of citizens. In 1835 the Alta California authorities set aside a 47,000-acre tract of pueblo land in San Diego to be used for the public's recreational purposes. This land included the site of present-day Balboa Park, making it one of the oldest places in the United States dedicated to public recreational usage.

No further activity took place until 1845, when a survey was done by Henry D. Fitch to map the 47,000 acres. The Mexican government was unable to develop a park due to the start of the Mexican-American War, and the resulting ceding of all Alta California including San Diego, to the United States in 1848.

Botanical Building, Balboa Park

On February 15, 1868, a request was put forth to the city's Board of Trustees to take two 160-acre plots of land, and create a public park. This request was made by one of the Trustees, E. W. Morse, who, along with real estate developer Alonzo Horton, had selected a site just northeast of the growing urban center of "New Town"—present day Downtown San Diego—for the nascent park's location.

The 1915 Panama–California Exposition design and development created much of the park's present day look and feel, and designed amenities. The Exposition celebrated the 1914 completion and opening of the Panama Canal, and to advertise that San Diego was the first U.S. port of call vessels encountered after passing through the canal and sailing north. A similar fair, the 1915 Panama–Pacific International Exposition, was held in "far to the north" San Francisco to celebrate the canal also. Although $5,000,000 had been set aside by Congress for celebrations of the Panama Canal opening, the majority of the funds went to the San Francisco expo. San Diego, with its considerably smaller population, was able to raise the funds it lacked through bonds approved by taxpayer votes. Exposition planning began in 1909 and the City Park was soon selected as the exposition site.

Balboa Park Golf Course

The Exposition's lead designer and site planner was architect Bertram Goodhue, well known for his Gothic Revival Style churches in New York and Boston, but looking for a regionally appropriate aesthetic to use in Southern California. Goodhue and associate architect Carleton Winslow chose to use the styles of highly ornamented Spanish Baroque architecture with the Spanish Colonial architecture created during the Spanish colonization era in New Spain-Mexico and the lower Americas, with Churrigueresque and Plateresque detailing "updating" the already popular Mission Revival Style—to create the Spanish Colonial Revival Style. The buildings and the style were extremely well received by the public and design professionals in California and nationally, becoming a reigning style for decades, and still the primary vernacular style in much of California. Goodhue's associate architect was Carleton M. Winslow, who is solely credited with the lattice-work Botanical Building and other structures. Goodhue's team, which included Kate Sessions and Lloyd Wright for landscape design, had won out over the local and more modernist Irving Gill to get the commission. One of the most significant improvements to the park from that time was the construction of the Cabrillo Bridge across a major canyon in the city. The bridge connects the main portion of the park with the western portion and with Laurel Street.

Poster, 1916 Exposition

On December 31, 1914, the Panama-California Exposition opened, with Balboa Park "crammed full" of spectators. President Woodrow Wilson pushed a telegraph button in Washington, D.C. to symbolically open the ceremonies by turning on the power at the park. Yellow and red were the themed colors of the event and were displayed throughout. All of the employees, workers, security people, and management staff were dressed in period Spanish and Mexican military uniforms, and much of the park was filled with plantings of exotic plants. Over 40,000 red Poinsettia plants, all in full bloom, were used. The event had been successful in attracting national attention. Even Pennsylvania's Liberty Bell made a brief three-day appearance in November 1915. The event's original 1915 run was such a success the fair was extended through 1916. Over the two years more than 3.7 million visitors were in attendance and a slight profit was earned over the total cost of organizing and hosting the expo. The surplus funds were donated to the San Diego Museum in the park. Several notable visitors during the two-year run included Henry Ford, William Jennings Bryan, Thomas Edison, Theodore Roosevelt, and William Howard Taft.

Post Card, 1915 Exposition

    Roosevelt, approving of the buildings' architecture, recommended that the "buildings of rare phenomenal taste and beauty" be left as permanent additions at Balboa Park. The majority of the buildings were only supposed to remain standing through 1916 and were not constructed with long-lasting materials. When the expo ended, several city discussions were held to determine what to do with the buildings. Goodhue recommended demolishing the buildings, saying "They are now crumbling, disintegrating and altogether unlovely structures, structures that lack any of the venerability of age and present only its pathos, and the space they occupy could readily be made into one of the most beautiful public gardens in the New World." Joseph W. Sefton, Jr., president of the Society of Natural History also called for their demolition, citing fire hazards: "All those old exposition buildings are nothing but fire traps. ... They are pretty to look at, but we may wake up any morning and find them gone, and our million dollars worth of exhibits with them." However, a city-appointed committee hired an architect to review the buildings, and he determined that the buildings could be restored by a slight margin over any costs to demolish the buildings. When the necessary funds and materials for restoration were donated by San Diegans and the labor was financed by the federal government, the buildings continued to remain in the park.

A new addition to the park during the post-war 1940s was the carillon in the California Tower (1946), which chimes the time every quarter hour. The San Diego Junior Theater, a program of the Old Globe Theatre was established in 1948, performing in the Prado Theatre. The amphitheater formerly known as the Ford Bowl became the Starlight Bowl, home of the Starlight Musical Theater (also known as the San Diego Civic Light Opera and as Starlight Opera), which performed Broadway musicals outdoors in the summer.

Balboa Park

    In 1959, the city hired an architectural firm to map out a plan for the park based on the suggestions of San Diegans along with the firm's recommendations. The initial review called for 13 of the original 1915 buildings to remain while replacing 11 others with new buildings in their place. The plan also called for adjusted roadways, additional landscaping, and improvements in parking. By 1967, the city and private charities such as the Committee of 100 undertook a major effort to restore the park's historic buildings. Most of the original Exposition buildings were continuing to deteriorate with some lacking foundations and minimal structural support. By the 1990s some of the Prado buildings were deteriorating so badly that "pieces of plaster regularly fell off the walls." Several crumbling buildings were torn down and replaced with permanent structures which were carefully detailed to maintain the original appearance. The Science and Education Building and the Home Economy Building were demolished to make room for the expansion of two new wings for the Timken Museum of Art. The loss of these two buildings along with the Casa de Balboa, the House of Charm, and the House of Hospitality, resulted in the formation of the independent organization, Committee of One Hundred, to attempt to preserve the exhibition buildings.

Several new museums opened during the 1960s and 1970s: the Timken Museum of Art in 1965, the Centro Cultural de la Raza in 1970, and the Reuben H. Fleet Science Center in 1973. The 1915–1916 exposition's Food and Beverage Building was rebuilt and reopened in 1971 as Casa del Prado.

Balboa Park, and the historic Exposition buildings, were declared a National Historic Landmark and National Historic Landmark District in 1977, and placed on the National Register of Historic Places. The following year two historic park structures burned down in two separate arson fires: the Aerospace Museum in the former Electric Building, and the 1935 Old Globe Theatre. The Aerospace Museum (now the San Diego Air and Space Museum) lost over $4 million in exhibits, and was reopened after moving into the old Ford Building. The Old Globe Theatre produced its 1978 season on a temporary outdoor stage, which was later upgraded to become one of the Globe's three theaters. The Old Globe Theatre itself was rebuilt and reopened in 1981. Queen Elizabeth II presented at the dedication ceremony for the theatre in 1983.

Throughout the 1980s, there were multiple reports throughout Balboa Park of vandalism, murder, rape, arson, and minor petty crimes. The resulting negative publicity during this period inspired Bruce Springsteen to write a song entitled "Balboa Park" focusing on the unpleasant aspects of the park. One of the Old Globe Theatre's starring actors was stabbed to death in the middle of the day in February 1985. A 36-year-old woman was gang-raped and murdered in the park in June 1986. To counter the increase in crime, city officials expanded police patrols in the park, and many of the individual museums hired security guards. After two murders in 1993 and the shooting of a young drama student walking across the Cabrillo Bridge in 1994, nighttime lighting in the park was increased, and video cameras were installed in several locations to allow park rangers and police to better monitor the area.

In 1998, the Reuben H. Fleet Science Center opened a larger building at its present location. The following year, the Hall of Champions Sports Museum moved to the old Federal Building.

Aerospace Museum, Balboa Park

By 2000, over 12 million people visited the park each year. Plans are in development for a year-long celebration of the centennial of the 1915–16 exposition, called the Balboa Park 2015 Celebration.

The Park's master plan calls for removing a 67-space parking lot from the Plaza de Panama in front of the San Diego Art Museum, and restoring it as a pedestrian-only plaza. In August 2010 a plan was unveiled by Mayor Jerry Sanders and philanthropist Irwin M. Jacobs to replace that parking with a two-level parking garage at the site of the current Spreckles Organ Pavilion parking lot. The plan also called for making the Cabrillo Bridge one-way, eastbound only, so that people could enter the park via the Cabrillo Bridge but could exit only via Park Boulevard. Instead of the current traffic route through the center of the Prado, inbound traffic would be deflected via a new bridge off ramp through the current Alcazar Gardens parking lot toward the new parking garage. The Alcázar Gardens parking lot would be for disabled parking only and for loading and unloading of passengers. The new parking garage would house 750–900 cars and would be landscaped on top.

Balboa Park

San Diego Zoo

The San Diego Zoo is a zoo in Balboa Park, San Diego, housing over 3,700 animals of more than 650 species and subspecies. It is also one of the few zoos in the world that houses the giant panda.

Panda, San DiegoZoo

The zoo offers a guided tour bus that traverses 75% of the park. There is an overhead gondola lift called the Skyfari, providing an aerial view of the zoo. The Skyfari was built in 1969 by the Von Roll tramway company of Bern, Switzerland.

Exhibits are often designed around a particular habitat. The same exhibit features many different animals that can be found side-by-side in the wild, along with native plant life. Exhibits range from an African rain forest (featuring gorillas) to the Arctic taiga and tundra in the summertime (featuring polar bears). Some of the largest free-flight aviaries in existence are here. Many exhibits are "natural" with invisible wires and darkened blinds (to view birds), and pools and open-air moats (for large mammals).

Gorilla, San Diego Zoo

The San Diego Zoo is one of the world's few major zoos to have almost all of its major exhibits be open-air; the only major exhibition building on grounds is the Reptile House.

The San Diego Zoo also operates the San Diego Zoo Safari Park, which displays animals in a more expansive setting than at the Zoo. Animals are regularly exchanged between the two locations, as well as between San Diego Zoo and other zoos around the world, usually in accordance with Species Survival Plan recommendations.

Koala, San DiegoZoo

The cool, sunny maritime climate is well suited to many plants and animals. Besides an extensive collection of birds, reptiles, and mammals, it also maintains its grounds as an arboretum, with a rare plant collection. As part of its gardening effort, it raises some rare animal foods. For example, the zoo raises 40 varieties of bamboo for the pandas on long-term loan from China, and it maintains 18 varieties of eucalyptus trees to feed its koalas.

Old Town

Old Town San Diego State Historic Park, located in the Old Town neighborhood of San Diego, is a state protected historical park. It commemorates the early days of the town of San Diego and includes many historic buildings from the period 1820 to 1870. The park was established in 1968. In 2005 and 2006, California State Parks listed Old Town San Diego as the most visited state park in California.

Old Town

On September 3, 1971, it was added to the National Register of Historic Places as Old Town San Diego Historic District.

Zorro

Johnston McCulley

1919

Zorro (Spanish for *Fox*) is the secret identity of Don Diego de la Vega (originally Don Diego Vega), a nobleman and master swordsman living in the Spanish colonial era of California. The typical image of him is a black-clad masked outlaw who defends the people of the land against tyrannical officials and other villains. Not only is he much too cunning and *foxlike* for the bumbling authorities to catch, but he delights in publicly humiliating those same foes.

Zorro's visual motif is typically a black costume with a flowing Spanish cape, a flat-brimmed Andalusian-style hat, and a black cowl mask that covers the top of the head from eye level upwards. Andalusia (Andalucía is an autonomous community of Spain. It is the most populous and the second largest in terms of land area.

Zorro

His favored weapon is a rapier which he often uses to leave his distinctive mark, a Z made with three quick cuts. A rapier is a relatively slender sharply pointed Sword, used mainly for thrusting attacks mainly in use in Europe in the 16th and 17th centuries He also uses a bullwhip, rather like the later Indiana Jones.

Zorro (often called *Señor* or *El Zorro*) debuted in McCulley's 1919 story *The Curse of Capistrano*. At the denouement, Zorro's true identity is revealed to all.

Douglas Fairbanks and Mary Pickford, on their honeymoon, selected the story as the inaugural picture for their new studio, United Artists, beginning the character's cinematic tradition. The story was adapted as *The Mark of Zorro* in 1920, which was a success. The Mark of Zorro is a silent motion picture released in 1920 starring Douglas Fairbanks and Noah Beery. McCulley's story was re-released by the publisher Grosset and Dunlap under the same title to tie in with the film.

Due to public demand fueled by the film, McCulley wrote over 60 additional Zorro stories starting in 1922. The last, *The Mask of Zorro* was published posthumously in 1959. These stories ignore Zorro's revealing his identity to everyone. The black costume that modern audiences associate with the character stem from Fairbanks' smash hit movie rather than McCulley's original story, and McCulley's subsequent Zorro adventures copied Fairbanks's Zorro rather than the other way around. McCulley died in 1958.

The Mark of Zorro

In *The Curse of Capistrano* Don Diego Vega becomes Señor Zorro in the pueblo of Los Angeles in California "to avenge the helpless, to punish cruel politicians", and "to aid the oppressed". He also robs from villains and gives to the poor, like Robin Hood. The story involves him romancing *Lolita Pulido*, an impoverished noblewoman. While Lolita is unimpressed with Diego, who pretends to be a passionless fop, she is attracted to the dashing Zorro. Other characters include *Sgt. Pedro Gonzales*, Zorro's enemy and Diego's friend; Zorro's deaf and mute servant *Bernardo*; his ally *Fray (Friar) Felipe*; his father *Don Alejandro Vega*, and a group of noblemen (*caballeros*) whom at first hunt him but are won over to his cause

In *The Curse of Capistrano* McCulley describes Diego as "unlike the other full-blooded youths of times"; though proud as befitting his class (and seemingly uncaring about the lower classes), he shuns action, rarely wearing his sword except for fashion, and is indifferent to romance with women. Zorro is a quite agile athlete and acrobat, using his bullwhip as a gymnastic accoutrement to swing through gaps between city roofs, and is very capable of landing from great heights and taking a fall. Although he is a master swordsman and marksman, he has more than once demonstrated his more than able prowess in unarmed combat, against multiple opponents.

His calculating and precise dexterity as a tactician has enabled him to use his two main weapons, his sword and bullwhip, as an extension of his very deft hand. He never uses brute strength, more his fox-like sly mind and well-practiced technique to outmatch an opponent. Zorro has a medium-sized dagger tucked in his left boot for emergencies. He uses his cape as a blind, a trip-mat--and when used effectively--a disarming tool. Zorro's boots are also sometimes weighted, as is his hat, which he has thrown, frisbee-like, as an efficiently substantial warning to enemies. Usually he uses psychological mockery to make his opponents too angry to be coordinated in combat.

Zorro is also a skilled horseman. His horse is *Tornado*.

Mission Bay

The wide marshland that once lured mariners to their doom at the mouth of the San Diego River has since been dredged and designated as an aquatic playground. Mission Bay Park covers 4,200 acres in roughly equal parts of land and water. A network of waterways, inlets and islets make the best way to explore Mission Bay by boat. Most of its 27 miles of meandering shoreline are sandy beaches, with the remainder devoted to marinas and resorts. The paramount symbol of watery fun in Mission Bay is SeaWorld in the southeast quadrant of the park. At Fiesta Island and Leisure Lagoon in the east bay, the names say it all, while it's easy to imagine what to expect at places like Sail Bay and Mariners Cove on the west end. There's always something happening in Mission Bay, from waterskiing and wakeboarding to sailing and swimming.

Areas of greatest interest and their associated uses within Mission Bay Park include: Vacation Isle with its resort hotel, Barefoot Bar and public parks; Crown Point a favorite spot for volleyball games; Ski Beach a hot spot for company parties and casual picnics; Santa Clara Point with its excellent Aquatic Center offering water sports rentals and instruction; Sail Bay with its wide running path, Fanuel Park playground, and nightly live music at the Catamaran Hotel; Mariners Point, home of the ESPN X-Games and the Bahia Hotel; Quivera Basin offering daily fishing and scuba diving charters, the Islandia Hotel and a sampling of waterfront shops and restaurants; Dana Landing the busy boat launching ramp and sportfishing center; East Mission Bay Park with its information center, endless grass parks, Hilton Hotel Resort, playgrounds and boat launching ramps; and Fiesta Island the multi-purpose, dune-covered island enjoyed by recreational enthusiasts of all kinds.

Mission Bay

Torrey Pines State Natural Reserve

     Torrey Pines State Natural Reserve is located within San Diego city limits and yet remains one of the wildest stretches of land on the Southern California coast. Because of the efforts and foresight of the people in this area, 2000 acres of land are as they were before San Diego was developed -with the chaparral plant community, the rare and elegant Torrey pine trees, miles of unspoiled beaches, and a lagoon that is vital to migrating seabirds. One can imagine what California must have looked like to the early settlers, or to the Spanish explorers, or even to the first California residents here, the Kumeyaay people.

Torrey Pines

There are 8 miles of trails, a visitor center, and guided nature walks on weekends and holidays. Torrey Pines is visited by travelers from all over the world and by local residents who come daily to rest at the stunning overlooks, walk a peaceful trail, or exercise in a clean, beautiful environment. Special care has been taken to preserve Torrey Pines State Natural Reserve and keep it that way now and forever.

The Torrey Pine, *Pinus torreyana*, is the rarest pine species in the United States, an endangered species growing only in San Diego County and on one of the Channel Islands, endemic to the coastal sage and chaparral ecoregion of California.

Del Mar Racetrack

Del Mar Racetrack is an American Thoroughbred horse racing track at the Del Mar Fairgrounds in the seaside city of Del Mar, 20 miles north of San Diego. Operated by the Del Mar Thoroughbred Club, it is known for the slogan: "Where The Turf Meets The Surf." It was built by a partnership including Bing Crosby, the actor Pat O'Brien, Jimmy Durante, Charles S. Howard and Oliver Hardy.

Del Mar Race Track

When Del Mar opened in 1937, Bing Crosby was at the gate to personally greet the fans. On August 12, 1938, the Del Mar Thoroughbred Club hosted a $25,000 winner-take-all match race between Charles S. Howard's Seabiscuit and the Binglin Stable's colt, Ligaroti. In an era when horse racing ranked second in popularity with Americans to Major League Baseball, the match race was much written and talked about and was the first nationwide broadcast of a Thoroughbred race by NBC radio. In the race, Seabiscuit was ridden by jockey George Woolf and Ligaroti by Noel Richardson. In front of a record crowd that helped make the fledgling Del Mar race track a success, Seabiscuit won an exciting battle by a nose.

By 1940, Del Mar became a summer playground for many Hollywood stars. Between 1942 and 1944 the facility was closed due to the Second World War. Initially, the grounds were used for training by the United States Marine Corp, then as a manufacturing site for parts to B-17 bombers.

The first Bing Crosby Handicap was held at Del Mar in 1946 and that same year the Sante Fe Railroad began offering a racetrack special bringing spectators, bettors and horses to Del Mar from Los Angeles. Throughout the late 1940s and 1950s the track became the Saratoga of the West for summer racing. The track had large purses for many stakes, over half of which were won by the legendary jockey, Bill Shoemaker.

San Diego Botanical Gardens

The San Diego Botanic Gardens, formerly Quail Botanical Gardens, is a botanical garden in Encinitas. At 37 acres, the garden includes rare bamboo groves (said to be the largest bamboo collection in the United States), desert gardens, a tropical rainforest, California native plants, Mediterranean climate landscapes, and a subtropical fruit garden. The gardens are open to the public daily. The name of the facility was changed in 2009 to better reflect the garden's status as a regional attraction.

Explore four miles of garden trails, enjoy restful vistas, flowering trees, majestic palms, and the nation's largest bamboo collection. Thanks to the mild climate, plants from all over the world thrive. The diverse topography provides a variety of microclimates giving the visitor a sensation of going from a desert environment to a tropical rainforest.

Until 1957 the gardens were the private estate of Ruth Baird Larabee, at which time she donated her house and grounds to the County of San Diego. The Quail Botanical Gardens Foundation was established in 1961.

Today the gardens include nearly 3,000 varieties of tropical, subtropical, and California native plants. Collections include the climate-based gardens for the New

World and Old World Desert, Coastal Sage Scrub, Sub-Tropical Fruit, a Pinetum, a Palm Canyon, as well as geographically organized gardens for Africa, Australia, Arid Madagascar Garden, Arid South America, the Canary Islands, Cape South Africa, Central America, the Himalayas, the Mediterranean, the Middle East, New Zealand, the Pan-Tropical Rainforest with a 60-foot waterfall, and the Pacific.

Plant varieties include fuchsias, hibiscus, bamboos, proteas, cacti and succulents, as well as other drought-resistant plants including Australian shrubs. Herbs, water plants, wildflowers, perennials, brugmansias, cork oaks, and palms are also featured.

Of particular interest is the maturing Cork Oak (*Quercus suber*) forest. Paths wind through a cluster of twisted and majestic trees whose bark has been used for making corks for thousands of years.

San Diego Botanical Garden

Carlsbad Flower Fields

For over sixty years, the rolling hills of Carlsbad have been a spectacular and coordinated display of natural color and beauty. The nearly fifty acres of Giant Tecolote Ranunculus flowers that make up The Flower Fields at Carlsbad Ranch are in a full bloom for approximately six to eight weeks each year - from early March through early May - literally bringing the famous fields back to life. This annual burst of color, which has become part of the area's local heritage, is also one of nature's official ways of announcing the arrival of spring.

Carlsbad Flower Fields

The blooming hillside was given the unofficial name, the "flower fields," by Carlsbad's residents, who began to consider it part of the local heritage. The practical name stuck, and became officially called The Flower Fields® in 1993.

Since 1993 The Flower Fields® have expanded to include displays of new spring flowers for your garden. These displays and the Artist Garden continue the tradition of bringing the joy and exuberance of color and nature to visitors.

California Surfing Museum

The Museum provides an inspiring and hip backdrop for its permanent and rotating exhibits. A mural of a perfect barrel caught just off the beach, south of Oceanside's famous pier, is the focal point for tourist snapshots.

California Surfing Museum

Known for its collection of surfboards dating back to the 1920s, the museum offers rotating exhibits and year-round events that include an annual Surf Festival in November.

Exhibits include an interesting compilation of Great Surfer/Shapers that recognizes and honors names through photos and memorabilia. Duke Kahanamoku, George Freeth, John Kelly, Tom Blake, Steve Lis, Simon Anderson and Loren Whitey Harrison are recognized names heralded through this tribute exhibit, one of many rotating exhibits that grace the walls of this corner shop that enjoys great window displays. Listed in travel guidebooks throughout the world, the California Surf Museum brings in over 17,000 visitors each year, making it a top tourist destination in downtown Oceanside. A trip to the museum is a must for anyone curious about surfing.

Marine Corps Base Camp Pendleton

Marine Corps Base Camp Pendleton is the major West Coast base of the United States Marine Corps and serves as its prime amphibious training base for Assault Craft Unit 5. It is located on the Southern California coast, in San Diego County, and bordered by Oceanside to the south, San Clemente, Cleveland National Forest, Orange and Riverside counties to the north, and Fallbrook to the east.

Camp Pendelton

    The base was established in 1942 to train U.S. Marines for service in World War II. By October 1944, Camp Pendleton was declared a "permanent installation" and by 1946, it became the home of the 1st Marine Division. It was named after Marine General Joseph Henry Pendleton (1860–1942), who had long advocated setting up a training base for the Marine Corps on the west coast. Today it is the home to myriad Operating Force units including the Marine Expeditionary Force and various training commands

    The base's diverse geography, spanning over 125,000 acres, plays host to year-round training for Marines in addition to all other branches of the U.S. military. Amphibious and sea-to-shore training takes place at several key points along the base's 17 miles of coastline. The main base is in the Mainside Complex, at the southeastern end of the base, and the remote northern interior is an impact area. Daytime population is around 100,000. Recruits from nearby Marine Corps Recruit Depot, San Diego spend a month on Pendleton's Edson Range receiving field training, and after graduating from boot camp return to the base's School of Infantry for further training. Camp Pendleton remains the last major undeveloped portion of the Southern California coastline, save for a few small state parks.

San Onofre Nuclear Generating Station

The San Onofre Nuclear Generating Station (SONGS) is a nuclear power plant located in the northwestern corner of San Diego County, south of San Clemente. The site is surrounded by the San Onofre State Park and sits next to highway Interstate 5. The landmark spherical containment buildings around the reactors are designed to prevent unexpected releases of radiation. The closest tectonic fault line is the Cristianitos Fault, which is considered inactive. The plant has been the site of many protests by anti-nuclear groups.

The facility is operated by Southern California Edison. Edison International, parent of SCE, holds 78.2% ownership in the plant; San Diego Gas & Electric Company, 20%; and the City of Riverside Utilities Department, 1.8%. The plant employs over 2000 people. The plant is located in Nuclear Regulatory Commission Region IV.

San Onofre Nuclear Generating Station

Western White House

In 1968 President Richard Nixon bought part of the H. H. Cotton estate, one of the original homes built by one of Hanson's partners. Nixon called it "La Casa Pacifica", but it was nicknamed the "Western White House", a term now commonly used for a President's vacation home. It sits above one of the West Coast's premier surfing spots, Trestles, and just north of historic surfing beach San Onofre. During Nixon's tenure it was visited by many world leaders, including Soviet Premier Leonid Brezhnev, Mexican President Gustavo Díaz Ordaz, Prime Minister of Japan Eisaku Sato, and Henry Kissinger, as well as businessman Bebe Rebozo.

Western White House

Section 2

California1

Dana Point to Long Beach
32 miles

California 1

State Route 1 (SR 1) is a major north-south state highway that runs along most of the Pacific coastline of California. Highway 1 has several portions designated as either Pacific Coast Highway (PCH), Cabrillo Highway, Shoreline Highway, or Coast Highway. Its southern terminus is at Interstate 5 (I-5) near Dana Point in Orange County and its northern terminus is at U.S. Highway 101 (US 101) near Leggett in Mendocino County. Highway 1 also at times runs concurrently with US 101, most notably through a 54-mile stretch in Ventura and Santa Barbara Counties, and across the Golden Gate Bridge.

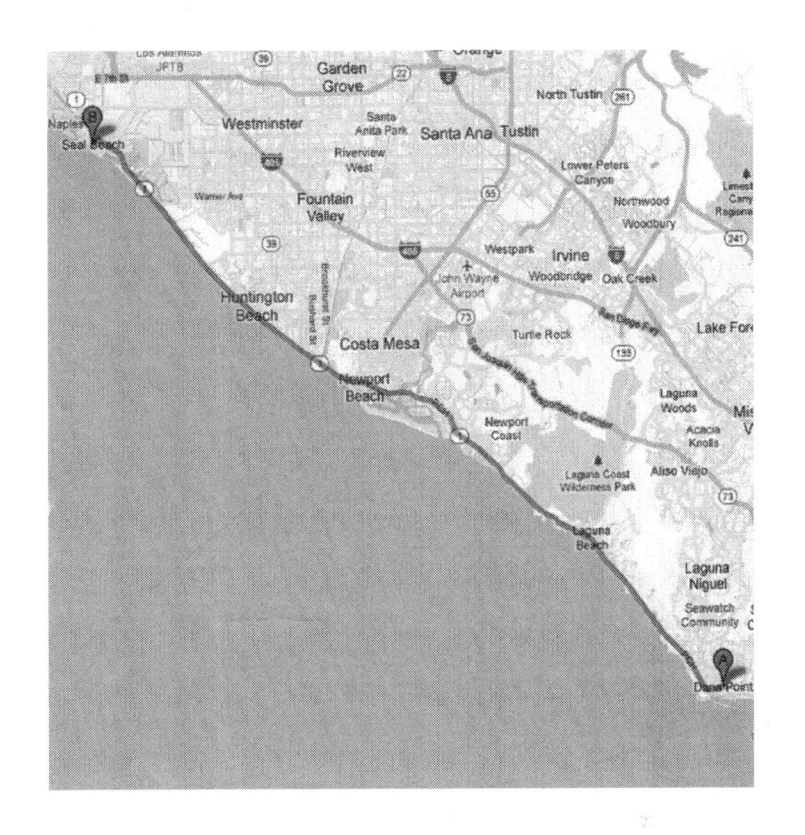

Dana Point to Long Beach (Google Maps)

CaliforniaHighway 1

    The highway is famous for running along some of the most beautiful coastlines in the USA, leading to its designation as an All-American Road. In addition to providing a scenic route to numerous attractions along the coast, the route also serves as a major thoroughfare in the Greater Los Angeles Area, the San Francisco Bay Area, and several other coastal urban areas. SR 1 was built piecemeal in various stages, with the first section opening in the Big Sur region in the 1930s. However, portions of the route had several names and numbers over the years as more segments opened. It was not until the 1964 state highway renumbering that the entire route was officially designated as Highway 1. Although SR 1 is a popular route for its scenic beauty, frequent landslides and erosion along the coast have caused several segments to either be closed for lengthy periods for repairs, or re-routed further inland.

Dana Point Harbor

Dana PointHarbor is not only a beautiful harbor in one of the most romantic areas of Californiait is also a bustling portside community, offering many amenities to both residents and guests. The Dana Point Harbor is divided into the East and West Basin, both of which operate as a separate marina. Combined, they have a total of 2,500 slips for vessels of various sizes. Included in the harbor are 50 guest slips for boats transiting the coastline and yacht clubs, which makes weekend cruises from the harbor ever more popular and exciting. Additional harbor facilities are a ten lane launch ramp, dry boat storage hoist, fishing pier, shipyard, marine fuel dock, three yacht clubs, and a commercial sports fishing operation, which offers whale watching trips throughout the year.

Dana PointHarbor

At the far west end of Dana PointHarbor, you'll find the Ocean Institute, which is a unique educational experience for children and adults alike. The Ocean Institute also displays the brig "Pilgrim" which is a full-sized replica of the square-rigged vessel on which Richard Henry Dana sailed into this cove. The Pilgrim is docked adjacent to the fishing pier and offers school children the experience of life aboard a sailing ship in the 19th century.

1000 Steps Beach

1000 Steps Beach is located between 9th & 10th streets in South Laguna Beach, features sand volleyball courts and nets at this tucked away beach which features very limited parking. Prominent features of this beach include surfing and volleyball via a steep set of stairs. Though there are not necessarily 1,000 steps at this beach (really about 230), who's counting when it seems so steep? Body surfing area, volleyball and a famous beach known for its long staircase leading to a spectacular surfing area are trademarks of this South Laguna Beach public beach. Like most Laguna Beaches, the beach itself is noticeable for its appearance as a friendly, neighborhood beach that's intimate and tucked away from view. Facilities at Thousand steps beach consist of a restroom and shower.

1000 Steps Beach

Pageant of the Masters

The Pageant of the Masters is an annual festival held by the Festival of Arts in Laguna Beach. The event is known for its *tableaux vivant* or "living pictures" in which classical and contemporary works of art are recreated by real people who are made to look nearly identical to the originals through the clever application of costumes, makeup, headdresses, lighting, props, and backdrops.

Pageant of the Masters

The first Festival of Arts occurred in 1932, and the first presentation of the Pageant occurred in 1933. Since then, the two events have been held each summer, apart from a four year interruption caused by World War II.

In 1933, at the second Festival of Arts, artist Lolita Perine had an idea for a living work of art. Convincing residents of Laguna Beach to dress in costume, she seated them behind an oversized frame, recreating well-known works of art. The "Spirit of the Masters Pageant" was formally started the next year by the Festival's organizers and was put on again in 1934, but in those early days was an amateurish operation. In 1934, local developer Roy Ropp expressed his dissatisfaction with the poor quality of the production in blunt terms; the Festival's board responded to his frank criticism by placing him in charge of the Pageant. He renamed it the "Pageant of the Masters" and with the assistance of his wife Marie, organized a high-quality and well-received production in the summer of 1935. Building upon this initial success, the Ropps continued to refine and improve the Pageant through its 1941 production; then the Festival and Pageant were suspended for four years due to World War II. Because of increasing personal friction between the Ropps and the Festival's board, Roy Ropp came back only once after the war to direct the Pageant, in 1950. He died in 1974, but today is still remembered as the "Father of the Pageant.

The Pageant is held eight weeks each summer and consists of 90 minutes of "living pictures" accompanied by a professional narrator, an orchestra, and period songs by professional vocalists. It hosts more than a quarter million people each year.

Balboa Island

Relaxed and charming, Balboa Island in Orange County, has a history rooted in land speculation, transportation and dance halls. In 1899, W.S. Collins, who had made his fortune in Southern California land speculation and transportation, was convinced to purchase 1000 acres of the land around the Newport Bay for development. At that time, Orange County was mostly orange groves and there were no rail lines leading into the area, and H.E. Huntington wasn't interested in building any. Collins bought that land for $50,000, dredged the harbor to create the man-made Balboa Island, connected it to Los Angeles via the Pacific Electric Railroad and within 15 years, property on Balboa Island was worth $5,000,000.

Balboa Pavilion

In 1905, the Balboa Pavilion was built and became the focal point of the Balboa Peninsula. It was originally built as a Victorian bath house and terminal for the Pacific Electric Red Car line, but soon was converted into a dance hall and became a destination throughout the southland for dancing and revelry. It was joined in the 20's by the Rendezvous Ballroom, Southern California's premier dance hall. All the "big bands" - Stan Kenton, Benny Goodman ,at King Cole, Dorsey Brothers, Harry James,Glenn Miller - played at the Rendezvous throughout the 30's and 40's.

The Balboa Pier was built in 1906 as a companion to the Balboa Pavilion. Land speculators wanted to attract lot buyers to undeveloped land on Balboa Island and the Balboa Peninsula, and when the Pacific Electric Railway opened up service to the Island, the pier and Pavilion were built as destinations for visitors. The plan worked and people came from all around Southern California to enjoy the beaches and many purchased lots and built vacation homes.

Balboa Harbor "Christmas Boat Parade"

The pier has become a popular place to fish, and the Harbor is known to be a good spot to catch flounder and mackerel. Also, starfish grow on the pier, feeding on mussels attached to the pilings and can often been seen when the tide is out.

In 1913, the "Illuminated Boat Parade" was started and eventually morphed into the "Christmas Boat Parade", which continues to this day. Hundreds of crafts bedecked with lights and ornaments participate in the annual Newport Harbor Christmas Boat Parade through the Harbor to the delight of thousands of viewers, culminating in a fireworks display over the Balboa Pavilion.

In 1919, Joe Beek, still a college student at the time, saw the possibilities for Balboa Island. He was granted permission to begin a ferry service between the Balboa Peninsula and the Island. Starting with one ferry - basically a large rowboat with a small motor - Joe began offering crossings for a nickel per person. He didn't have a regular ferry schedule; instead folks who needed to cross the harbor made an appointment over the telephone. Today, the Beeks family still runs the Balboa Island Ferry. They now have multiple ferries, in continuous service, that carry up to 3 cars, as well as passengers.

Balboa Ferry

In 1936, the Balboa Fun Zone was created on the boardwalk and the ferris wheel, with its views of the Newport Harbor, has become one of the premier landmarks of Balboa Island. In 1986, the Fun Zone was completely re-vamped and today, the carousel, bumper cars, delicious food and great shopping make it a favored destination.

These days, Balboa Island is known as a charming destination for locals and visitors alike. Strolling the waterfront boardwalk, enjoying the games and rides at the Balboa Pavilion, relaxing on sun-filled beaches or fishing from the Balboa Pier, there is plenty to do and enjoy on Balboa Island.

The O.C.

The O.C. is an American teen drama television series that originally aired on the Fox television network in from August 5, 2003, to February 21, 2007, running a total of four seasons. The series, created by Josh Schwartz, portrays the fictional lives of a group of teenagers and their families residing in the affluent seaside community of Newport Beach.

Newport Beach

California playlist

A call for the songs that best evoke Southern California results in some wide-ranging responses.

By PETER LARSEN / The Orange County Register

We opened up the request lines and asked you for your favorite Southern California songs - tunes that with just a few notes or words make you think, Ah, yes - *this* is where I live. From almost every point on our imaginary radio dial you responded: Rock, rap, punk, surf, big band, folk, country - even Hawaiian - songs all got votes. Jazz fans, you let us down.

Your favorite California songs

For one, you do love your place- named ditties, don't you? Twenty songs featured "California in the title, and votes also went to places such as "Beverly Hills" (Weezer), "Garden Grove" (Sublime), "Santa Catalina" (the Four Preps) and "Santa Barbara" (Ronny Milsap).

The sunny side of Southern California life surfaced in a tsunami of beach songs: "**Surf City,**" (Jan and Dean), "Surfin' Safari" (the Beach Boys), "Catch a Wave" (the Beach Boys again), and "Warmth of the Sun" (more Beach Boys!).

The dark side of life got votes, too, with "Desperados Under the Eaves" (Warren Zevon), "Welcome to the Jungle" (Guns N' Roses) and "Life in the Fast Lane" (the Eagles).

And there were people: "L.A. Woman" (the Doors), "California Man" (the Move; Cheap Trick), and "Boyz-N-the-Hood" (Eazy-E).

And now, the results!

In first place, a tie! Between songs that couldn't be much more different if they tried: **"Ventura Highway"** by '70s soft rock outfit America and **"California Love"** by late rapper Tupac Shakur.

In second, another tie! Between two '60s classics: **"California Dreamin'"** by the Mamas & the Papas, and **"California Girls"** by the Beach Boys.

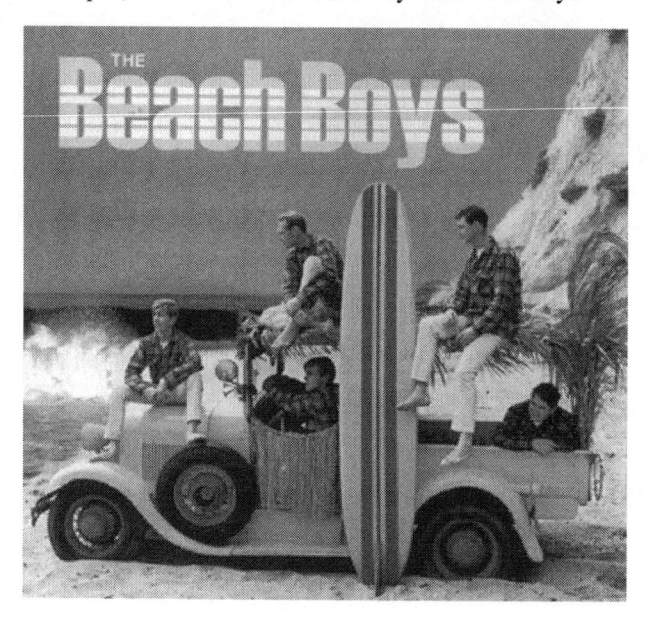

Beach Boys

In third place, **"I Love L.A."** by Randy Newman, **"L.A. Woman,"** by the Doors, and **"Surf City** by Jan & Dean.

In fourth place. **"Hotel California"** by the Eagles, **"Surfin' USA,"** by the Beach Boys, and **"Californication"** by the Red Hot Chili Peppers.

And in fifth place, **"California"** by Joni Mitchell, **"California Sunset"** by Neil Young, **"Estimated Prophet"** by the Grateful Dead, **"Going Back to Cali"** by LL Cool J, **"Going to California"** by Led Zeppelin, **"It Never Rains (in Southern California),"** by Albert Hammond, and **"To Live and Die In L.A.,"** by Tupac Shakur. All with three votes.

For complete results, see www.ocregister.com/Life. To hear why some of you picked the songs you did, read on.

"Ventura Highway," America, 1972

"The sunny Southern California weather, heading to the beach at the drop of a hat. I didn't have a convertible, but with the windows open and as many girls as you could cram in your big Buick, heading down to Zuma Beach - that's what it reminds me of.

"I hear it on the radio and the memories come back."

- Katy Morgan, 45, Laguna Beach

"After a particularly grueling basketball practice one evening, a bunch of us piled into the Kooiman brothers' old Chevy wagon, thankful for a ride home. They had a pair of cheap speakers hooked up in the back compartment where I was stretched out, and 'Ventura Highway' came on.

"I don't know if it was the fatigue or the company of good friends under those particular circumstances, but the sound and the faces are one of the most indelible memories of my lifetime, and the song has remained a siren call of life in Southern California for me ever since."

- Scott Borzi, 49, Huntington Beach

"California Love," Tupac Shakur, 1995

"This song is about how much of a fun state California is, especially Southern California. This song to me is exactly how I picture California, the Golden State, the state that knows how to have fun."

- Mario La Cascia, 17, Gilbert West High School, Buena Park

"The lyrical meaning of the song is that California knows how to party. The whole point is that you should have fun, a sun-filled, wild and rockin' state. To me this song is just cruising down Crenshaw Boulevard, and feeling that sunshine."

- Alain Gonzalez, 17, Gilbert West High School, Buena Park

Mamas and Papas

"California Dreamin'," the Mamas & the Papas, 1966

"Growing up in the Philadelphia area during the '60s, I heard a lot of songs about the California lifestyle. Songs about girls, surfing, cars and the beach. But none sticks in my head like 'California Dreamin'!' Walking to school on those cold, gray and snowy Philly days, freezing my you-know-what off, I would hear those lyrics and wish that one day I would move to the warm West Coast."

- Joe Fazio, 53, Aliso Viejo

"California Girls," the Beach Boys, 1965

"'California Girls' made California a place where everyone wanted to come and see. It brings back some great '60s memories. I was in the service, going to Vietnam, and that was one of the things I brought with me, a Beach Boys album. That kind of brought me closer back to home all the time."

- Allen Barker, 58, Irvine

"I Love L.A.," Randy Newman, 1983

"I think 'I Love L.A.' is the perfect Calisong. It describes the whole L.A. basin and it's such a cheerful song. Every time I hear it, I can't help but sing it out loud."

- Cord Blank, 34, Fountain Valley

"California Nights," Lesley Gore, 1967

"As a young boy in Illinois during the '60s, every time I heard this song I wanted to steal my dad's car and drive to California I'm sure you'll get entries for all of the famous songs, but listen to this song and see if it doesn't feel like Southern California."

- Ed Buchner, 51, Placentia

"Burritos ," Sublime, 1996

"The rhythm immediately invokes the distinct SoCal Nineties phenomenon of third-wave ska. The lyrics reveal the essentials of surfer life: burritos, porn, pot and lazy days in bed."

- Ian Alloway, 27, Irvine

"California Man," the Move, 1972

"This song transcends anything that the Eagles have done just in sheer jubilation. The Eagles are just too self-absorbed and serious. They make me want to move OUT of California!

- William Heideman, 52, Garden Grove

"California 1," Con Funk Shun, 1981

"I have found that my favorite times in California have been on or near 'California 1.' I went to school at Pepperdine in Malibu - on California 1. I married my sweetie in Palos Verdes at the Wayfarers Chapel (OK, a little off California 1). Our first vacation was up California 1 to Big Sur and Monterey. Our first house was in Laguna Beach, a couple of blocks off California 1.

"We now live in Newport Beach on Lido and can see California 1 from the swings at the park where I take my 4 1/2-year-old daughter. Anyway, like the song, 'California 1' is the highway of my memories, spinnin' me toward my dreams."

- John Taylor, 44, Newport Beach

"Good Time Charlie's Got the Blues," Danny O'Keefe, 1972

"What a song! You had to be, at 33, thinking about your future in Edmonton, Alberta, Canada (or some other godforsaken place) with all the weird crap that destroys your well-being to appreciate this song. ... It was minus-35 degrees for three months and 'leavin' for L.A.' sounded like the right place to go to feel bad - at least you felt warm. I am here now at 54 loving every minute of it, and I thank Danny for planting the seed."

- Ron Glatley, 54, Mission Viejo

"Diamonds On My Windshield," Tom Waits, 1974

"Not all of us have lil' deuce coupes or convertible BMWs. This is a great nighttime driving song describing the trip up the 5 from San Diego to Hollywood circa 1975 (probably in a car that would just make it). You should give it extra credit for the Orange Drive-In reference."

- Rob Beck, 48, Costa Mesa

"Boyz-N-The-Hood," Eazy-E, 1987

"Now I live in a nice house in Anaheim, but before I lived in Compton. This song represents where I came from because I saw the killing, the abusive relationships that my neighbors had, the drugs, the hustling after school, and most importantly, the gang life I was exposed to. To me, this song means Southern Cali because Cali is not a sunset, a nice song about positives. To me it's about goin' day by day and being happy that as the day goes by it might be a good day."

    - Yolanda Macias, 16, Gilbert West High School, Buena Park

"Low Rider," War, 1975

"'**Low Rider**' on my iTunes makes me smile, bob my head, feel very cool ... and, by the way, the album cover is a classic hoot! And I gotta admit, I've often wondered if some dynamic hydraulics on my Honda Civic's fanny could reach a respectable altitude!"

    - Jane Davison, 72, Tustin

"Where It's At," Beck, 1996

"Cali summer and funky white boy shuffle is a left coast standard."

    - Bob Macias, 49, Mission Viejo

"When the Swallows Come Back to Capistrano," various, 1939

"The ultimate in Southern California romance songs might well be Leon Rene's 'When the Swallows Come Back to Capistrano.' This song has mission bells, a lost love and cute little birdies, all with an Orange County setting and chords that are really tough to play. Plus it was a big hit. Ink Spots and Glenn Miller both had top 10 hits with it!"

    - Joe Richman, 53, Orange

"You're So Vain," Carly Simon, 1972

"Captures the essence of Southern California plastic smiles, plastic surgery, plastic degrees, plastic fitness, plastic diets and overvalued real estate, save for the Getty Museum, without which we'd be the cultural unwashed armpit of the world."

    - Mike Nally, 59, Garden Grove

"Harbor Lights," Claude Thornhill Orchestra, 1937

"As a very young girl, I grew up in Kansas and my eyes saw not much more than fields of wheat. Our family finally moved to California and for the first time I saw the most amazing sight, the Pacific Ocean. We settled in Costa Mesa and I attended my wonderful high school, Newport Harbor. I spent my days with my friends and boyfriends in both Newport and Balboa, and in the late '30s the song 'Harbor Lights' became popular.

"During my high school days and dating boyfriends, we'd often stroll hand in hand along the shore as the moon created a soft glow across the waves. Squishing our bare toes in the sand, we'd stop and wonder in awe at the romantic sight cast by the many harbor lights. Thus, the song 'Harbor Lights' became our song.

"Several years ago, I found myself once again walking along the Balboa Pier with an old high school friend. As we stopped and saw the many lights shining upon the shore, the flood of memories brought back to mind that once-again beautiful song from my school days, 'Harbor Lights.'"

- Linnell Cordell, 83, Santa Ana

"Life in the Fast Lane," the Eagles, 1976

"Reason why: The pace is very fast here in California and you don't get time to stop and smell the roses. Traffic is horrible, and no one gets to enjoy the beautiful mountains and gorgeous beach areas."

- Lillian Rossi, 63, Laguna Hills

"Hotel California," the Eagles, 1976

"This song has many different interpretations. My opinion is that California is this great big sparkling place where people go looking for wealth and glory. It is a great life, just like the hotel, but then it gets stressful. A lot of times people become drug addicts and alcoholics. People wake up one day and find themselves drugged out and screwed up. Before you know it, you're stuck. There's no way out.

"That's what I think the Eagles were talking about. The beauty of California and how it leads to this crazy, addictive life."

- Sarah Delgado, 16, Gilbert West High School, Buena Park

"**MacArthur Park**," Richard Harris, 1968

"Forget the 'fun and sun' California songs of the Beach Boys. Songs of alienation and despair comprise my (picks). Number one is 'MacArthur Park.' What's sadder than 'a cake left out in the rain'? Melodramatic, but memorable."

- Dennis Petticoffer, 47, Orange

Surf City USA

Huntington Beach is a seaside city in Orange County. According to the 2010 census, the city population was 189,992; making it the largest beach city in Orange County in terms of population. It is bordered by the Pacific Ocean on the southwest, by Seal Beach on the northwest, by Costa Mesa on the east, by Newport Beach on the southeast, by Westminster on the north, and by Fountain Valley on the northeast.

Huntington Beach (aka HB) is known for its long 8.5-mile stretch of sandy beach, mild climate, excellent surfing and beach culture. The ocean waves are enhanced by a natural effect caused by the edge-diffraction of open ocean swells around the island of Catalina. Swells generated predominantly from the North Pacific in Winter and from a combination of Southern Hemisphere storms and hurricanes in the Summer focus on Huntington Beach creating consistent surf all year long thus giving HB the title 'Surf City', USA'.

Huntington Beach, "Surf City USA"

    Huntington Beach hosts the annual Surf City Surf Dog competition, raising money for animal charities while letting dogs strut their stuff in a costume contest, a one-mile walk, and of course, a surfing competition. There were two surfing heats: GROMS, where dogs could have as many volunteers in the water as possible to help, and SHREDDER, where dogs were judged on "the length of their ride, the size of the wave and their confidence on the board" and could only have two helpers.

Huntington Beach

Bolsa Chica Wetlands

    When entering the Bolsa Chica wetlands in Huntington Beach, look right (south) for two sand islands where California Least Terns and Snowy Plovers nest. Bolsa Chica Ecological Reserve offers free parking and admission. Bikes, horses and dogs are not permitted on the trail.

    163 pairs of Endangered Belding's Savannah Sparrows live, breed and nest at Bolsa Chica. Look for rare Light-footed Clapper Rails which have recently been spotted. On any day, you might see Great Blue Herons, Snowy Egrets, White and Brown Pelicans, Avocets and Black-necked Stilts, to name a few. In the fall and winter seasons, Lesser Scaups, Red-Breasted Mergansers, Ruddy Ducks and Common Loons come to visit. Tours are given on Saturday mornings.

Bolsa Chica Wetlands

Huntington Beach Oil Feld

The Huntington Beach Oil Field is part of rich pools of oil found along the West Coast in the early 1920s stretching from Huntington Beach, to Santa Barbara.

Huntington Beach Oil Field

On May 24, 1920, the first Huntington Beach well, the Huntington A-1 was brought in as a producing well. By October 1921, the field had 59 producing wells. Even with 16 of those 59 wells being idle, the field produced 16,500 barrels a day, with each well producing from 50 to 200 barrels daily.

Seal Beach Naval Weapons Station

Best known for its long wooden pier and Main Street charm, Seal Beach has a new claim to fame today: The Seal Beach Naval Weapons Station was named the navy's best small base in the world. Officially named the winner of the 2012 Navy Installation Excellence Award for Small Installations, the base beat out every other small base for its environmental stewardship, efficiency and personnel.

Seal Beach Naval Weapons Station

Section 3

California 1 to Interstate 710 to Interstate 110 to California 1

Los Angeles County
82 miles

Los Alamitos Bay

Los Alamitos Bay in Long Beach, is one of California's great hidden secrets, though during the summer when the cars come to a complete stop, trying to find a place to park, you'll not believe it. The southernmost beach city includes communities within its bounds such as Alamitos Bay. It is part of the community of Belmont Shore and faces Naples Island, or Naples, another community in Long Beach.

Winters are paradise in the bay with its stretches of sand overlooking multi-million dollar properties with private docks along the Long Beach peninsula, Belmont Shore and Naples Island. In the bay you'll see sailboats, kayaks, gondolas, swimmers, kids and at play and a love of the water, beaches and sun-kissed skin that's tanned by the California rays.

Alamitos Bay is a body of water adjacent to the Pacific Ocean. Naples Island and the Long Beach peninsula both are on the Alamitos Bay.

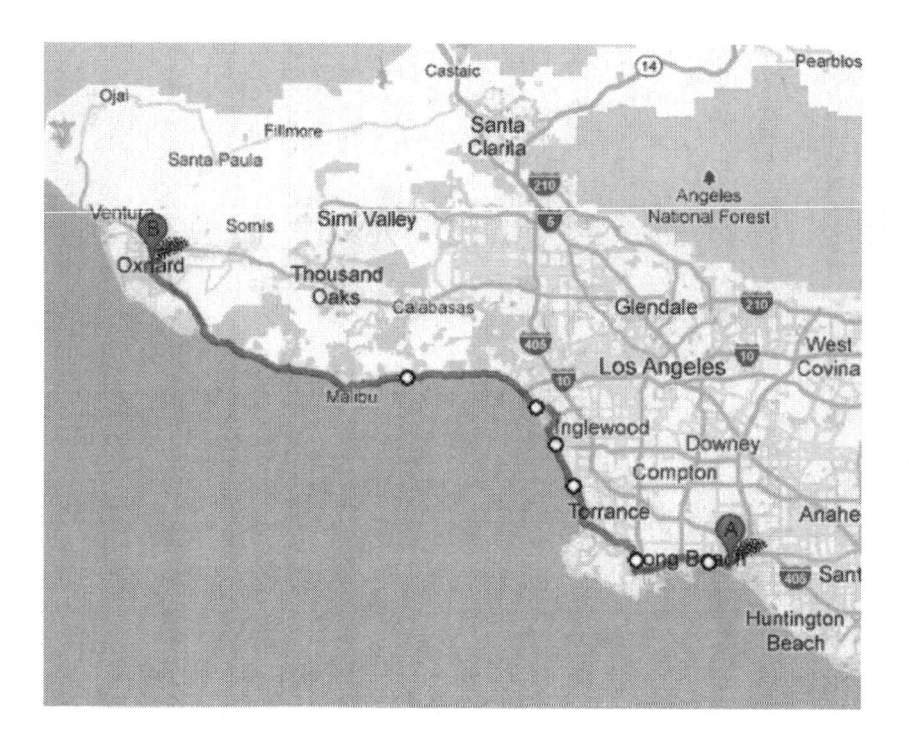

Los Angeles County (Google Maps)

Los Alamitos Bay

Long Beach Harbor

      The Port of Long Beach, also known as Long Beach's Harbor Department, is the second busiest container port in the USA after the Port of Los Angeles, which it adjoins. Acting as a major gateway for U.S.-Asian trade, the port occupies 3,200 acres of land with 25 miles of waterfront in the city of Long Beach. The Port of Long Beach is located less than two miles southwest of Downtown Long Beach and approximately 25 miles south of downtown Los Angeles. The seaport boasts approximately $100 billion dollars in trade and provides more than 300,000 jobs in Southern California. The twin ports of Los Angeles and Long Beach are, together, the single largest source of air pollution in the metropolitan Los Angeles area. Both ports have implemented a number of environmental programs to reduce pollution levels while continuing port growth.

Long Beach Harbor

Long Beach Grand Prix

The Toyota Grand Prix of Long Beach is an open-wheel race held on a street circuit in Long Beach. Christopher Pook is the founder and promoter which began as a vision while working at a travel agency in downtown Long Beach. It was the premier circuit in the Champ Car from 1996, and was the first event in the World Series each year from 2004. The 2008 race was the last race for Champ Cars as the series merged with the Indy Racing League, and is now an event on the Izod IndyCar Series calendar.

The Long Beach Grand Prix in April is the single largest event in the city of Long Beach. Attendance for the weekend regularly reaches or exceeds 200,000 people.

Long Beach Grand Prix

The Long Beach Grand Prix is the longest running major "street" race held on the North American continent. It started in 1975 as a Formula 5000 race on the streets of downtown, and became a Formula One event the following year.

The current race circuit is a 1.968-mile temporary road course carved out of the city streets surrounding the Long Beach Convention Center which actually doubled as the pit paddock during the days of Formula One. The circuit also goes primarily over the former location of The Pike historic amusement zone. It is particularly noted for its last section, which sees a hairpin turn followed by a long, slightly curved front straightaway which runs the length of Shoreline Drive. The circuit is situated on the Long Beach waterfront, and is lined with palm trees (especially along the front straightaway), making for a scenic track.

Aquarium of the Pacific

The Aquarium of the Pacific (formerly the Long Beach Aquarium of the Pacific) is an aquarium on a 5-acre site on Rainbow Harbor in Long Beach. The Aquarium sees 1.5 million visitors a year and has a total staff of over 900 people including more than 300 employees and about 650 volunteers.

Aquarium of the Pacific

The Aquarium features a collection of over 11,000 animals representing over 500 different species. It focuses on the Pacific Ocean in three major permanent galleries, sunny Southern California and Baja, the frigid waters of the Northern Pacific and the colorful reefs of the Tropical Pacific. Popular exhibits include the interactive Shark Lagoon (guests can pet sharks and sting rays) and Lorikeet Forest (guests can feed nectar to colorful lorikeet birds). Exhibits introduce the inhabitants and seascapes of the Pacific, while also focusing on specific conservation messages associated with each region. Exhibits range in size and capacity from about 5,000 to 350,000 gallons.

Queen Mary

RMS *Queen Mary* is a retired ocean liner that sailed primarily in the North Atlantic Ocean from 1936 to 1967 for the Cunard Line (known as Cunard-White Star when the vessel entered service). Built by John Brown & Company in Clydebank, Scotland, *Queen Mary* along with her running mate, the RMS *Queen Elizabeth*, were built as part of Cunard's planned two-ship weekly express service between Southampton, Cherbourg, and New York City. The two ships were a British response to the superliners built by German and French companies in the late 1920s and early 1930s. *Queen Mary* was the flagship of the Cunard Line from May 1936 until October 1946 when she was replaced by *Queen Elizabeth*.

Queen Mary

Queen Mary sailed on her maiden voyage on 27 May 1936 and captured the Blue Riband in August of that year; she lost the title to the SS *Normandie* in 1937 and recaptured it in 1938, and then held it until 1952. With the outbreak of World War II, she was converted into a troopship and ferried Allied soldiers for the duration of the war. Following the war, *Queen Mary* was refitted for passenger service and along with *Queen Elizabeth* commenced the two-ship transatlantic passenger service that the two ships were initially built for. The two ships dominated the transatlantic passenger transportation market until the dawn of the jet age in the late 1950s. By the mid-1960s the ship was ageing and though still among the most popular transatlantic liners, was operating at a loss.

After several years of decreased profits for Cunard Line, *Queen Mary* was officially retired from service in 1967. The ship left Southampton for the last time on 31 October 1967 and sailed to the port of Long Beach, where she remains permanently moored.

When *Queen Mary* was bought by Long Beach, the new owners decided not to preserve her as an ocean liner. It had been decided to clear almost every area of the ship below "C" deck (called "R" deck after 1950, in order to lessen passenger confusion, as the restaurants were located on "R" deck) to make way for the museum. This would increase museum space to 400,000 square feet. It required removal of all the boiler rooms, the forward engine room, both turbo generator rooms, the ship stabilisers and the water softening plant. The ship's now empty fuel tanks were then filled with local mud which would keep the ship's centre of gravity and draft at the correct levels, as these critical factors had been affected by the removal of all various components and structure. Only the aft engine room and "shaft alley", at the stern of the ship, would be spared. Remaining space would be used for storage or office space. One problem that arose during the conversion was a dispute between land-based and maritime unions over conversion jobs. The United States Coast Guard had final say; *Queen Mary* was deemed a building, since most of her propellers had been removed and her machinery gutted. The ship was also repainted with its red water level paint at a slightly higher level than previously. During the conversion, the funnels were removed as it was the only practical way to lift out the scrap materials from the engine and boiler rooms. It was subsequently found that the funnels were held together with 101 coats of paint, and they had to be replaced with replicas.

With all of the lower decks nearly gutted from R deck and down, Diners Club, the initial lessee of the ship, was to convert the remainder of the vessel into a hotel. During this conversion, the plan was to convert most of her first and second class cabins on A and B decks only into hotel rooms, and convert the main lounges and dining rooms into banquet spaces. On Promenade Deck, the starboard promenade deck would be enclosed to feature an upscale restaurant and cafe called Lord Nelson's and Lady Hamilton's themed like early 19th century sailing ships. The famed and elegant Observation Bar was redecorated as a western themed bar.

Cabin, Queen Mary

The smaller first class public rooms, such as the Drawing Room, Library, Lecture Room and the Music studio, would be stripped of most of their fittings and converted to commercial use, heavily expanding the retail presence on the ship. Two more shopping malls were built on the Sun Deck in separate spaces previously used for first class cabins and engineers' quarters.

Long Beach Harbor Light

Long Beach Harbor Light looks different from a traditional lighthouse. Labeled the "robot light" when established in 1949, it is completely automated and was the forerunner of the new version of 20th-century lighthouses on America's West Coast. The 42-foot high white, rectangular tower with a columnar base, features a 36-inch airway-type beacon and is controlled by the ANRAC system from the Los Angeles Harbor Light. The three-story facility, of monolithic design, is built of concrete supported on six cement columns cast into six pockets of a crib. In its commanding position in San Pedro's middle breakwater, the lighthouse was considered an uncanny mechanical wonder when first established. Later, another navigation light in the Long Beach area was erected atop the pilot station at the Port of Long Beach in 1968. Marking the harbor entrance channel, the light is accompanied by one of the United States Coast Guard's radar scanners.

Long Beach Harbor Light

Oil Islands

White Island is one of the oil islands. Named Freeman, Grissom, White, and Chaffee after the first four NASA astronauts to die in the line of duty.

These are artificial islands which house oil and gas production equipment. The artificial facades are designed to disguise the facility. In fact, there are active oil wells and pump jacks throughout Long Beach, LA, and the vicinity that are hidden beneath facades, in warehouses, fake houses, and other clever hiding places. Most residents don't know they live in the middle of active oil and gas production.

White Island

Vincent Thomas Bridge

    The Vincent Thomas Bridge is a 1,500-foot long suspension bridge, opened in 1963, crossing the Los Angeles Harbor, linking San Pedro, Los Angeles, with Terminal Island. The bridge is signed as part of State Route 47. It is named for California Assemblyman Vincent Thomas of San Pedro. It is the fourth longest suspension bridge in California. It is also the bridge with the 76th longest span in the world. The clear height of the navigation channel is approximately 185 ft.

    The bridge was built to replace the ferries that connected San Pedro and Terminal Island, in anticipation of increased traffic volume accompanying growth of the port. State legislator Vincent Thomas, representing San Pedro, was the bridge's champion. A special act of the legislature was required in order to name the bridge after Thomas while he was still in office.

Vincent Thomas Bridge

Throughout the bridge's construction and in the early years after its opening, it was derided as a "bridge to nowhere". In the 1970s, however, its importance drastically increased as the ports of Los Angeles and Long Beach displaced those of the San Francisco Bay Area as the principal port on the U.S. West Coast. Today, the Vincent Thomas Bridge carries a considerable volume of truck traffic from the southernmost slips of the Port of Los Angeles, in San Pedro, onto the Terminal Island Freeway and eventually to the southern end of the Long Beach Freeway; from there, freight goes from the port complex to the rail yards of East Los Angeles and the Inland Empire.

Korean Bell of Friendship

The Korean Bell of Friendship is a massive bronze bell housed in a stone pavilion in Angel's Gate Park, in the San Pedro neighborhood of Los Angeles. Located at the corner of Gaffey and 37th Streets, the section of the park is alternatively called the "Korean-American Peace Park," and occupies part of the former Upper Reservation of Fort MacArthur. The "Belfry of Friendship" (*Ujeong-ui Jonggak*) houses the bell.

Korean Bell of Friendship

The bell was presented by the Republic of Korea to the American people to celebrate the bicentennial of the United States and to symbolize friendship between the two nations. The effort was coordinated by Philip Ahn, a Korean-American actor. It was dedicated on October 3, 1976 and declared Los Angeles Historic-Cultural Monument No. 187 in 1978.

It is modeled after the Divine Bell of King Seongdeok the Great of Silla (also known as the Emille Bell), cast in 771 for Bongdeok Temple and now located at the National Museum of Gyeongju; both are among the largest bells in the world. The bell is made of over 17 tons of copper and tin, with gold, nickel, lead, and phosphorus added to the alloy for tone quality. It has a diameter of 7½ feet, average thickness of 8 inches, and a height of 12 feet. The exterior surface is richly decorated in relief, featuring four pairs of figures. Each pair includes a "Goddess of Liberty" (bearing some resemblance to the Statue of Liberty) and an *Seonyeo* or Korean spirit figure holding a Korean national symbol: a Taegeuk symbol, a branch of rose of Sharon, a branch of laurel, and a dove.

Southern California Live Steamers

The S.C.L.S. established in 1948, in Mrs. Lewis' (Founder of Little Engines) back yard, in Lomita CA, began laying track and operating at Wilson Park as early as 1986.

The S.C.L.S. mission is to educate the public about our rich railroad history and promote interest in the hobby. All members are City of Torrance Park and Recreation Volunteers. S.C.L.S. is very fortunate to have the generous support of the City of Torrance and our community riders. Wilson Park, Torrance CA, is located on Crenshaw Blvd. between Sepulveda Blvd. and Carson St.

Southern California Live Steamers

S.C.L.S. gives on average 1800-2000 rides, each run day. Visitors wishing to volunteer (i.e. Boy and Girl Scout projects) or become members, please check in at the table under the tent with station personnel. The Southern California Live Steamers is funded completely by it's members and the donations received during our public run days..Visitors from other Live Steam clubs are welcome to run their engines, however are not allowed to pull public passengers due to some tight curves (less than 60'). S.C.L.S. regularly operates a 4-6-2 Pacific and 2-6-0 and 2-4-4T N.G. Steam locomotives as well as GP38 and SW-1500 diesel locomotives.

Los Angeles International Airport

Los Angeles International Airport (LAX) is the primary airport serving the Greater Los Angeles Area, the second-most populated metropolitan area in the United States. It is most often referred to by its airport code LAX, with the letters pronounced individually. LAX is located in southwestern Los Angeles along the Pacific coast in the neighborhood of Westchester, 16 miles from the downtown core and is the primary airport of Los Angeles World Airports (LAWA), an agency of the Los Angeles city government formerly known as the Department of Airports.

Los Angeles International Airport

In 2011, LAX was the eighth busiest airport in the world after Hartsfield-Jackson Atlanta International Airport, Beijing Capital International Airport, London Heathrow Airport, Suvarnabhumi Airport, Chicago O'Hare International Airport, Dubai International Airport, and Tokyo Haneda International Airport with 61,862,052 passengers.

LAX is the busiest airport in the Greater Los Angeles Area, but other airports including Bob Hope Airport, John Wayne Airport, Long Beach Airport, and LA/Ontario International Airport also serve the region. LAX is also the busiest airport in California and the U.S. West Coast in terms of flight operations, passenger traffic and air cargo activity, leading it to be referred to as the "Gateway to the Pacific Rim."

In 1928, the Los Angeles City Council selected 640 acres in the southern part of Westchester as the site of a new airport for the city. The fields of wheat, barley and lima beans were converted into dirt landing strips without any terminal buildings. It was named Mines Field for William W. Mines, the real estate agent who arranged the deal. The first structure, Hangar No. 1, was erected in 1929 and is listed on the National Register of Historic Places.

Mines Field was dedicated and opened as the official airport of Los Angeles in 1930, and the city purchased it to be a municipal airfield in 1937. The name was officially changed to Los Angeles Airport in 1941, and to Los Angeles International Airport in 1949. The main airline airports for Los Angeles had been Burbank Airport (then known as Union Air Terminal, and later Lockheed Field) and the Grand Central Airport in Glendale. By 1940 most airlines served Burbank only; in late 1946 most airline flights moved to LAX, but Burbank always retained a few.

Mines Field did not extend west of Sepulveda (California 1). It was rerouted in 1950 to loop around the west ends of the extended east-west runways (now runways 25L and 25R), which by November 1950 were 6,000 feet long. A tunnel was completed in 1953 allowing Sepulveda Boulevard to revert to straight and pass beneath the two runways; it was the first tunnel of its kind. For the next few years the two runways were 8,500 feet long. On July 10, 1956 Boeing's 707 prototype (the 367-80) visited LAX. The *Los Angeles Times* said it was its first appearance at a "commercial airport" outside the Seattle area.

The April 1957 Official Airline Guide showed 66 weekday departures on United Airlines, 32 American Airlines, 32 Western Airlines, 27 TWA, 9 Southwest, 5 Bonanza Air Lines and 3 Mexicana Airlines; also 22 flights a week on Pan American World Airways and 5 a week on Scandinavian Airlines (the only direct flights to Europe).

LAX Tunnel

    In 1958 the architecture firm Pereira & Luckman was contracted to design a master plan for the complete re-design of the airport in anticipation of the "jet age." The plan, developed along with architects Welton Becket and Paul Williams, called for a massive series of terminals and parking structures to be built in the central portion of the property, with these buildings connected at the center by a huge steel-and-glass dome. The plan was never realized, and shortly thereafter the Theme Building was constructed on the site originally intended for the dome.

    The distinctive white "Theme Building", designed by Pereira & Luckman architect Paul Williams and constructed in 1961 by Robert E. McKee Construction Co., resembles a flying saucer that has landed on its four legs. A restaurant with a sweeping view of the airport is suspended beneath two arches that form the legs. The Los Angeles City Council designated the building a cultural and historical monument in 1992. A $4 million renovation, with retro-futuristic interior and electric lighting designed by Walt Disney Imagineering, was completed before the "Encounter Restaurant" opened there in 1997. Tourists and passengers are able to take the elevator up to the roof of the "Theme Building", which closed after the September 11 attacks for security reasons and reopened to the public on weekends beginning on June 10, 2010.

LAX Theme Building

American Airlines' 707-123s flew the first jet passengers out of LAX to New York in January 1959; the first wide-body jets were TWA's Boeing 747s to New York in early 1970. All terminals were originally satellite buildings out in the middle of the tarmac, reached by underground tunnels from the ticketing area.

In 1981 the airport began a $700 million expansion in preparation for the 1984 Summer Olympics. To streamline traffic flow and ease congestion the U-shaped roadway leading to the terminal entrances was given a second level, with the lower level for arriving passengers and the upper level for departing. Connector buildings between the ticketing areas and the satellite buildings were added, changing the gate layout to a "pier" design and completely enclosing the facilities. Two new terminals (Terminal 1 and the International Terminal) were constructed and Terminal 2, then two decades old, was rebuilt. Multi-story parking structures were also built in the center of the airport.

On July 8, 1982, groundbreaking for the two new terminals were conducted by Mayor Tom Bradley and World War II aviator General James Doolittle. The $123 million, 963,000-square-foot International Terminal was opened on June 11, 1984, and named in Bradley's honor.

On April 29, 1992 the airport was closed for violence and cleanups after the 1992 Los Angeles Riots over the Rodney King beating. The airport was closed again on January 17, 1994 due to the Northridge earthquake.

LAX Pylons

In 2000, before Los Angeles hosted the Democratic National Convention, fifteen glass pylons up to ten stories high were placed in a circle around the intersection of Sepulveda Boulevard and Century Boulevard, with additional pylons of decreasing height following Century Boulevard eastward, evoking a sense of departure and arrival. Conceived by the designers at Selbert Perkins Design, the towers and 30 foot "LAX" letters provide a gateway to the airport and offer a welcoming landmark for visitors. Illuminated from the inside, the pylons slowly cycle through a rainbow of colors that represents the multicultural makeup of Los Angeles and can be customized to celebrate events, holidays or a season. This was part of an overall face-lift that included new signage and various other cosmetic enhancements that was led by Ted Tokio Tanaka Architects. The LAX pylons underwent improvements in 2006, as stage lighting inside the cylinders was replaced with LED lights to conserve energy, make maintenance easier and enable on-demand cycling through various color effects.

Starting in the mid-1990s under Mayors Richard Riordan and James Hahn, modernization and expansion plans for LAX were prepared, only to be stymied by a coalition of residents who live near the airport. They cited increased noise, pollution and traffic impacts of the project. In late 2005, newly elected Mayor Antonio Villaraigosa was able to reach a compromise, allowing some modernization to go forward while encouraging future growth among other facilities in the region.

It is illegal to limit the number of passengers that can use an airport; however, in December 2005 the city agreed to limit their construction of passengers gates to 163. Once passenger usage hits 75 million, a maximum of two gates a year for up to five years will be closed, which theoretically will limit maximum growth to 79 million passengers a year. In exchange, civil lawsuits were abandoned, to allow the city to complete badly needed improvements to the airport.

On March 19, 2007 the Airbus A380 made its debut at LAX, landing on runway 24L. Though LAX was originally supposed to be the first US city to see the A380, Airbus later decided to forgo LAX in favor of New York's JFK. After city officials fought for the super-jumbo jet to land at LAX, the A380 landed simultaneously in New York's JFK airport and LAX.

Before the 1930s, existing airports used a two-letter abbreviation based on the weather stations at the airports. At that time, "LA" served as the designation for Los Angeles Airport. But with the rapid growth in the aviation industry the designations expanded to three letters c. 1947, and "LA" became "LAX." The letter "X" has no specific meaning in this identifier. "LAX" is also used for the Port of Los Angeles in San Pedro and by Amtrak for Union Station in downtown Los Angeles.

LAX Bag Tag

Loyola Marymount University

Loyola Marymount University (LMU) is a comprehensive co-educational private Roman Catholic university in the Jesuit and Marymount traditions located in Los Angeles. The University is one of 28 member institutions of the Association of Jesuit Colleges and Universities and one of five Marymount institutions of higher education.

As of 2010, Loyola Marymount is one of the largest Roman Catholic universities on the West Coast with just over 9,000 undergraduate, graduate and law school students.

Loyola Marymount University

LMU sits atop a bluff area 150 acres in the Westchester area of West Los Angeles located in the Del Rey Hills. The original 99 acres were donated to the university by Harry Culver. Xavier Hall, named for St. Francis Xavier, S.J., a companion of St. Ignatius of Loyola, S.J., and St. Robert's Hall, named for St. Robert Bellarmine, S.J., a cardinal and Doctor of the Church, were the first two buildings to be built on the current Westchester Campus. Following their completion in 1929, Xavier Hall housed both the Jesuit Faculty and the students at the time while St. Robert's Hall served as the academic and administrative building.

Loyola Marymount University traces its history through Loyola University, founded in 1911 as the successor to St. Vincent's College which was founded in 1865, and Marymount College, founded in 1933 with its roots in Marymount School which was founded in 1923. Loyola Marymount, which sits atop the bluffs overlooking Marina Del Rey and Playa Del Rey is the parent school to Loyola Law School located in downtown Los Angeles.

Loyola Marymount University Quad

    Sacred Heart Chapel and the Regents Bell Tower were the next non-residential structures to be built on the campus (1953–1955). The Malone Student Center, named for Lorenzo M. Malone, S.J., an alumnus of the university and former Dean of Students and Treasurer of the University, was completed in 1958 and renovated in 1996. LMU now houses 36 academic, athletic, administrative, and event facilities as well as 12 on-campus residence halls (dormitory and suite models) and six on-campus apartment complexes[2].

---

[2] Editor's note: The editor's oldest daughter Attended Loyola Marymount University from 1986 until she graduated in 1990. She went on to receive her teaching credential

The campus houses four large open grass areas not reserved exclusively for athletic play. Alumni Mall and Sunken Gardens provide scenery to the campus that is already laden with views of the entire Los Angeles Basin, Marina del Rey, Playa Vista, Playa del Rey, and the Pacific Ocean.

Loyola Marymount University

The university's acquisition of University Hall in 2000 brought the campus a new entrance as well as much-needed office and classroom space. University Hall is a facility unique to any academic institution. It was originally constructed for Hughes Aircraft as their world headquarters and converted from an exclusively corporate facility to a building thriving with academic life. LMU acquired the 1,000,000-square-foot building in January 2000 from Raytheon, which bought Hughes Aircraft. LMU completed the interior remodel of approximately 250,000 square feet in April 2001. The building, which houses the university's Bellarmine College of Liberal Arts, is constructed of steel and concrete and is divided into seven structures above ground. University Hall has over 500,000 square feet of floor space and contains over 1,000 parking spaces in three underground levels. The 70,000 square feet of atrium space is and will continue to be the venue for many LMU events. University Hall was featured

---

from San Jose State University. She has been a high school a English teacher ever since.

in season one, episode two of the television series "Bones", as the fictional "Hamilton Cultural Center" in Washington, D.C.

The *Princeton Review* has recently ranked LMU as having the 7th most beautiful campus in America *CampusSqueeze* college e-zine ranked LMU as having the 3rd most beautiful campus in America.

Playa Del Rey Incline Railway

This incline railway was the partner of Angels Flight in downtown Los Angeles. Two cars ran in a counter balance configuration from a Los Angeles Pacific Railway stop at the base of the Westchester cliffs to a hotel at the top of the bluff. The line only existed from about 1901-1909. The incline eventually succumbed to unstable soils and cliff erosion. The two cars were named 'Alphonse' and 'Gaston'.

Playa Del Rey Incline Railway

Marina Del Rey

    Marina del Rey is a seaside unincorporated area and census-designated place (CDP) in Los Angeles County. Its Fisherman's Village offers a view of Marina del Rey's dominant feature as it is the world's largest man-made small craft harbor, with 19 marinas with capacity for 5,300 boats and is home port to approximately 6500 boats.

Marina del Rey

Prior to its development as a small craft harbor, the land occupied by Marina Del Rey was a salt-marsh fed by freshwater from the Ballona Creek, frequented by duck hunters and few others. Burton W. Chase, a member of the Los Angeles County Board of Supervisors, referred to the area as mud flats, though today the area would more properly be referred to as wetlands.

In the mid-19th century, M.C. Wicks thought of turning this Playa del Rey estuary into a commercial port. He formed the Ballona Development Company in 1888 to develop the area, but three years later the company went bankrupt.

In 1916, the U.S. Army Corps of Engineers revisited the idea of a commercial harbor, but declared it economically impractical. In 1936 the U.S. Congress ordered a re-evaluation of that determination, and the Army Corps of Engineers returned with a more favorable determination; however, the Marina del Rey harbor concept lost out to San Pedro as a commercial harbor and development funding went to the Port of Los Angeles instead.

In 1953, the Los Angeles County Board of Supervisors authorized a $2 million loan to fund construction of the marina. Since the loan only covered about half the cost, the U.S. Congress passed and President Dwight D. Eisenhower signed Public Law 780 making construction possible. Ground breaking began shortly after.

Marina del Rey

With construction almost complete, the marina was put in danger in 1962–1963 due to a winter storm. The storm caused millions of dollars in damage to both the marina and the few small boats anchored there. A plan was put into effect to build a breakwater at the mouth of the marina, and the L.A. County Board of Supervisors appropriated $2.1 million to build it. On April 10, 1965 Marina del Rey was formally dedicated. The total cost of the marina was $36.25 million for land, construction, and initial operation.

St. Monica Catholic High School

St. Monica Catholic High School traces its origin to the turn of the century when the Sisters of the Holy Names of Jesus and Mary, at the request of Bishop Montgomery, first opened a small elementary school in 1899. In 1901, to meet the need for more facilities and a potential high school, the sisters erected the "Academy of the Holy Names" which stood at the corner of Third and Arizona Streets. The Academy housed both an elementary school and a high school until 1930 when the elementary school became the "St. Monica Parish Elementary School" and was transferred to its present site on Seventh Street.

After five years it became apparent that even more facilities would be needed for the Academy's high school. The Sisters, at the request of the pastor Monsignor Nicholas Conneally, sold the Academy building in the fall of 1935 and consented to staff a parish high school. St. Monica Catholic High School opened at its present location in September of 1937. Accommodating both boys and girls, the school's faculty consisted of five sisters and two priests with the first graduating class numbering twenty: seventeen girls and three boys.

St. Monica High School

    The school grew rapidly at the new location and both additional facilities and faculty were needed. The Brothers of Mary came in to teach the boys from 1946 to 1948, at which time the Brothers of St. Patrick took over this job, arriving from Ireland and establishing their first house in the United States. The sisters retained instruction of the girls.

    Facilities were expanded in May of 1956 when, under the direction of Msgr. Raymond O'Flagherty, ground was broken for the new building on Lincoln Boulevard in order to house the Boys' Department. The Girls' Department would remain in today's West Wing[3].

---

[3] Editor's Note: Patricia A. Brown attended St. Monica Catholic High School from 1957 until her graduation in 1961. She met the author in 1962. They married in 1965,and have been happily married ever since.

In the fall of 1968, for the first time since 1946, classroom instruction became "co-ed". In 1970 the two faculties, student bodies and administrations merged under the leadership of Sister Michaeline Mary, SNJM. In June of 1977 the Brothers of St. Patrick decided they could no longer help staff the school and departed.

Today, more than 100 years after the Sisters of the Holy Names' arrival, their educational ministry continues at St. Monica Catholic High School. Fulfilling the needs of Catholic students of Santa Monica and the west side of Los Angeles, St. Monica stands as a monument to the struggles and vision of the many religious, priests, and lay persons who are dedicated to the Christian instruction of youth.

Muscle Beach

Located just south of the Santa Monica Pier is the original location of Muscle Beach. Known as "The Birthplace of the Physical Fitness Boom of the Twentieth Century", Muscle Beach is a longtime landmark in the world of bodybuilding and the workout area dates back to the 1930's. The network of outdoor workout equipment is where celebrities such as Kirk Douglas and Mae West and famous fitness guru Jack LaLanne and other internationally known bodybuilders trained.

Fully restored and refurbished, Muscle Beach serves gymnasts, acrobats and youth with an extensive gymnastics training area. Other features include chinning bars at various heights, parallel bars, rings, a small jungle gym for children and a padded gymnastics area.

Muscle Beach

    Francois Henri "Jack" LaLanne (September 26, 1914 - January 23, 2011) was an American fitness, exercise, and nutritional expert and motivational speaker who is sometimes called "the godfather of fitness" and the "first fitness superhero." He described himself as being a "sugarholic" and a "junk food junkie" until he was 15. He also had behavioral problems, but "turned his life around" after listening to a public lecture by Paul Bragg, a well-known nutrition speaker. During his career, he came to believe that the country's overall health depended on the health of its population, writing that "physical culture and nutrition — is the salvation of America.

Jack LaLanne

    Decades before fitness began being promoted by celebrities like Jane Fonda and Richard Simmons, LaLanne was already widely recognized for publicly preaching the health benefits of regular exercise and a good diet. He published numerous books on fitness and hosted a fitness television show between 1951 and 1985. As early as 1936, at age 21, he opened one of the nation's first fitness gyms in Oakland, California which became a prototype for dozens of similar gyms using his name. One of his 1950s television exercise programs was aimed toward women, whom he also encouraged to join his health clubs. He invented a number of exercise machines, including leg-extension and pulley devices. Besides producing his own series of videos, he coached the elderly and disabled to not forgo exercise, believing it would enable them to enhance their strength.

    LaLanne also gained recognition for his success as a bodybuilder, as well as for his prodigious feats of strength. Arnold Schwarzenegger once stated, "That Jack LaLanne's an animal!," after LaLanne, at 54, beat a 21-year-old Schwarzenegger "badly" in an informal contest. On the occasion of LaLanne's death, Schwarzenegger credited LaLanne for being "an apostle for fitness" by inspiring "billions all over the world to live healthier lives," and, as governor of California, had earlier placed him on his Governor's Council on Physical Fitness.

He was inducted to the California Hall of Fame and has a star on the Hollywood Walk of Fame.

Santa Monica Pier

Santa Monica has had several piers over the years, however the current Santa Monica Pier is actually two adjoining piers that long had separate owners. The long, narrow Municipal Pier opened September 9, 1909, primarily to carry sewer pipes beyond the breakers, and had no amenities. The short, wide adjoining Pleasure Pier to the south, a.k.a. Newcomb Pier, was built in 1916 by Charles I. D. Looff and his son Arthur, amusement park pioneers.

Carousel, Santa Monica Pier

The Carousel was built in 1922 on the Pleasure Pier and features 44 hand-carved horses. It was rebuilt in 1990 inside the Looff Hippodrome. A calliope provides musical accompaniment.

The La Monica Ballroom opened in 1924 and closed in 1962. The La Monica Ballroom was the home of Spade Cooley television broadcasts in the early fifties. In 1955, the ballroom became the Hollywood Autocade housing over 100 unusual cars. From 1958 until 1962 it served as a roller skating rink, first as Skater's Ballroom and then Santa Monica Roller Rink. The speed skating club won many state and regional championships. The bridge to the pier and entry gate was built in 1938 by the federal Works Project Administration, and replaced the former grade connection.

The Looff Pier, then known as Newcomb Pier, was acquired by the city in the 1953. In the 1960s various plans were proposed that would entail removal of the pier. The strangest one called for the construction of an artificial island with a 1500-room hotel. It was approved by the City Council, but citizens formed "Save the Santa Monica Bay" to preserve the pier. The outstanding order to raze the pier was revoked by the city council in 1973. That same year the Carousel and Hippodrome were memorable sets in the film *The Sting*, although the story was set in Chicago.

Santa Monica Pier

In the 1950s Enid Newcomb suggested to family friend Morris "Pops" Gordon that his two sons, George and Eugene, purchase and operate the Pier's arcade. It didn't take much persuasion, for the Gordons instantly took to the Pier and ultimately made Playland Arcade into the Pier's longest running enterprise offering the day's contemporary games alongside those of yesterday, providing inexpensive entertainment to a diverse crowd. George's daughters Marlene and Joanie have kept the business within the family, and the next generation of Gordons is already in training to maintain the family tradition.

Palisades Park

Stretching 1.5 miles, Palisades Park offers the most scenic views of Santa Monica's 26 parks and is one of the best sunset destinations in Los Angeles County. The city's biggest park runs along Ocean - from Colorado Ave. to San Vicente - and features a Visitors Center kiosk, ☐picnic areas, benches, a Camera Obscura, ☐a rose garden, a pergola and a beacon overlook. Also located at Palisades Park is the ☐Senior Center (at Ocean and Santa Monica), and the nearby shuffleboard courts. Palisades Park is a City of Santa Monica Landmark and runs along the final stretch of the current course for the Los Angeles Marathon.

Palisades Park

Malibu

     Malibu is an affluent beachfront city in northwestern Los Angeles County. As of the 2010 census, the city population was 12,645. Malibu consists of a 21-mile strip of prime Pacific coastline. Nicknamed "the 'Bu" by surfers and locals, the community is famous for its warm, sandy beaches, and for being the home of many Hollywood movie stars and others associated with the entertainment industry. Signs around the city proclaim "27 miles of scenic beauty", referring to Malibu's original length of 27 miles before the city was incorporated in 1991.

Malibu

Most Malibu residents live within a few hundred yards of Pacific Coast Highway (State Route 1), which traverses the city, with some residents living up to a mile away from the beach up narrow canyons, and many more residents of the unincorporated canyon areas identifying Malibu as their hometown. The city is also bounded (more or less) by Topanga Canyon to the East, the Santa Monica Mountains consisting of Agoura Hills, Calabasas, and Woodland Hills to the North, the Pacific Ocean to the South, and Ventura County to the West.

Malibu's beaches include Surfrider Beach, Zuma Beach, Malibu State Beach, Topanga State Beach Point Dume State Beachand Dan Blocker Beach its local parks include Malibu Bluffs Park (formerly Malibu Bluffs State Park), Trancas Canyon Park Las Flores Creek Park and Legacy Park with neighboring parks Malibu Creek State Park, Leo Carrillo State Beach and Park, Point Mugu State Park, and the Santa Monica Mountains National Recreation Area, and neighboring state beach Robert H. Meyer Memorial State Beach that was once part of Old Malibu (before Malibu became a city), and better known as pristine beaches, El Pescador, La Piedraand El Matador

Zuma Beach

Malibu Colony was one of the first areas inhabited after Malibu was opened to the public in 1929 and it is one of Malibu's most famous districts. It is located south of Malibu Road and the Pacific Coast Highway, west of Malibu Lagoon State Beach, and east of Malibu Bluffs Park (formerly a state park). Initially May Rindge kept control of Malibu Beach, allowing a few wealthy Hollywood stars to build vacation homes. Nearly a decade later, money woes forced Rindge to sell the land, and the Colony was born. Long known as a popular private enclave for wealthy celebrities, the Malibu Colony today is a gated community, with multi-million dollar homes on small lots. The Colony commands breathtaking views of the Pacific Ocean, affording a spectacular coastline view stretching from Santa Monica to Rancho Palos Verdes to the south (known locally as the *Queen's Necklace*) and the bluffs of Point Dume to the north.

One of the most problematic side-effects of the fires that periodically rage through Malibu is the destruction of vegetation, which normally provides some degree of topographical stability to the loosely packed shale and sandstone hills during periods of heavy precipitation. Rainstorms following large wildfires can thus cause a phenomenon known as mudslides, in which water-saturated earth and rock moves quickly down mountainsides, or entire slices of mountainside abruptly detach and fall downward.

Malibu Mud Slide

Mudslides can and do happen at any time in Malibu, whether or not there has been a recent fire or rainstorm. Pacific Coast Highway, Kanan-Dume Road, and Malibu Canyon road (as well as many other local roads) have all been subject to many subsequent mudslide-related closures. During any period of prolonged or intense rain, Caltrans snowplows will patrol most canyon roads in the area, clearing mud, rocks, and other fallen debris from the roadways. Such efforts keep most roads passable, but it is nevertheless common for one or more of the major avenues in and out of Malibu to be temporarily shut down during the rainy season.

The Getty Villa Malibu

After 8 years and $275 million in renovations, the magnificent Getty Villa is receiving guests again. This former residence of oil tycoon J. Paul Getty, built in 1974 on the edge of a Malibu bluff with dazzling views of the ocean, was modeled after a first-century Roman country house buried by the eruption of Mount Vesuvius in A.D. 79 -- the Villa dei Papiri in Herculaneum, Italy. In fact, as you enter the sun-filled inner courtyard, it's not hard to imagine toga-clad senators wandering the gardens where fountains and bronze busts occupy the same spots as the original villa.

Getty Villa

The museum's permanent collection of Greek, Roman, and Etruscan artifacts -- dating from 6500 B.C. to A.D. 400 -- consists of more than 1,200 works in 23 galleries arranged by theme, and five additional galleries for changing exhibitions. Exhibits on display range from everyday items such as coins, jewelry, and sculpture to modern interactive exhibits that illustrate key moments in the history of the ancient Mediterranean. Highlights include *Statue of a Victorious Youth,* a large-scale bronze discovered in an Adriatic shipwreck that is kept in a special climate-controlled room to preserve the metal (it's one of the few life-size Greek bronzes to have survived to modern times), as well as a beautiful 450-seat open-air theater where visitors are encouraged to take a break. Performances of either a Greek comedy or tragedy take place here every September (a commanding rendition of *Elektra* featured Olympia Dukakis). For keeping the kids entertained, the Villa's education team created a hands-on space called the Family Forum where children can partake in art-related activities.

Section 4

The Central Coast

Oxnard to Santa Cruz

359 miles

Channel Islands National Park

Channel Islands National Park is a United States national park that consists of five of the eight Channel Islands off the coast of California, in the Pacific Ocean. Although the islands are close to the shore of densely-populated Southern California, their isolation has left them relatively undeveloped. The park covers 249,561 acres of which 79,019 acres are owned by the federal government. The Nature Conservancy owns and manages 76% of Santa Cruz Island, the largest island in the park.

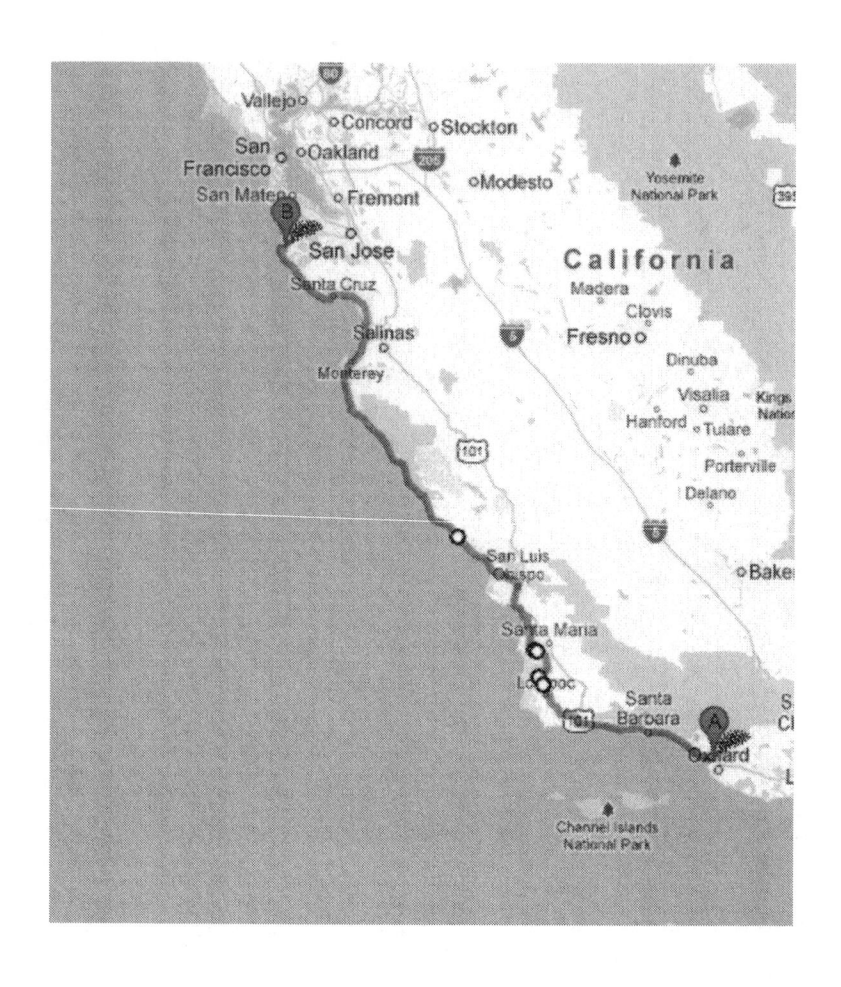

Oxnard to Santa Cruz (Google Maps)

Channel Islands

Channel Islands National Park is home to a wide variety of significant natural and cultural resources. It was designated a U.S. National Monument on April 26, 1938, and a National Biosphere Reserve in 1976. It was promoted to a National Park on March 5, 1980.

The islands within the park extend along the Southern California coast from Point Conception near Santa Barbara to San Pedro, a neighborhood of Los Angeles. Park headquarters and the Robert J. Lagomarsino Visitor Center are located in the city of Ventura.

The park consists of 249,354 acres, half of which are under the ocean, and includes the islands of:

- San Miguel 9,325 acres

- Santa Rosa 52,794 acres
- Anacapa 699 acres
- Santa Barbara 639 acres
- Santa Cruz 60,645 acres 76% owned by the Nature Conservancy, 24% by the National Park Service

Channel Islands

More than 2,000 species of plants and animals can be found within the park. However only three mammals are endemic to the islands, one of which is the deer mouse (*Peromyscus maniculatus*) which is known to carry the sin nombre hantavirus. Spotted Skunk and Channel Islands Fox also are endemic. The Island fence lizard is also endemic to the Channel Islands. Other animals in the park include Island Scrub Jay, harbor seal, California sea lion, island fox, spotted skunk, island night lizard, barn owl, American kestrel, horned lark and meadowlark and California brown pelican. One hundred and forty-five of these species are unique to the islands and found nowhere else in the world. Marine life ranges from microscopic plankton to the endangered blue whale, the largest animal ever to live on earth. Archeological and cultural resources span a period of more than 10,000 years.

Gray Whales

The oldest human remains in North America dating to 13,000 B.C., were discovered in 1959 on Santa Rosa Island.

The Channel Islands were created by tectonic forces, which caused them to rise up out of the ocean five million years ago. They have always been islands separate from the mainland, and thus have unique plants and animals found nowhere else on Earth.

Ventura Bus Stop

Since 2002 the Ventura Bus Stop at Telegraph Rd next to the Pacific View Mall remains as Ventura's most controversial piece of public art. Created by renowned sculptor, Dennis Oppenheim, "Bus Home " is a looping cork screw of steel, concrete, acrylic, paint, and electric light. It stands 36' at its tallest height.

Ventura Bus Stop

Per the artist: "The work depicts the metamorphosis of a bus becoming a house...entering the ground and coming up again. For the tired and often alienated traveler the experience of waiting wished to be intervened by the realization that the transaction will be complete. The passengers will arrive at their destination. They will arrive home."

Nearly ten years later, "Bus Home" decorates the north end of the Pacific View Mall as a monument of 21st century art and doing its best to remind riders they'll soon be home. Love it or hate it, the bus stop often makes the list of the most cool or unusual bus stops around the world. However, most Venturans have yet to warm up to this "funky" bus stop.

Rincon

Rincon is tucked slightly off Highway 101/California 1, between La Conchita and Carpinteria. There are no hamburger stands, no souvenir shops, no proclamations that you have arrived. What you'll find is authentic surfing that anyone visiting California to surf must put on their list of experiences. Its fame is legendary as are the surfers who have driven or hitched a ride to this location. They come from around the globe to surf Rincon, possibly mainland America s top surfing destination. Some say its been a popular spot for 100 years or more. Open between 6 a.m. and 9 p.m. daily, the park sits next to gated beach houses that enjoy views of the ocean and world-class surfing.

Rincon

You can't fully appreciate the magnitude of surfing in California until you visit Rincon Point. As you drive your vehicle into either of two parking lots exiting the 101 at Bates Road, an eery scene reminds non-surfers of the film, March of the

Penguins. Dressed mostly in black, wetsuited guys and girls dominate the scene. Looking like seals or penguins on a mission, the percentage of surfers in one place is so overwhelming that it hits you between the eyes as you realize that Rincon is where surfing lives and legends are created.

Santa Barbara Polo Club

Founded in 1911, the Santa Barbara Polo Club in Santa Barbara, is the premiere equestrian Polo club in the Western United States. The club, located between the foothills of the Santa Ynez Mountains and the Pacific Ocean, consists of three full size outdoor polo fields, one arena, extensive horse boarding and exercise facilities, as well as stabling for 350 horses. The Santa Barbara Polo Club is home to the Pacific Coast Open, United States Polo Association (USPA) America Cup and the USPA Circuit Player's Cup[4].

---

[4] Editor's Note: In the spring of 1965, the Editor's fraternity held it's annual spring dance at the Santa Barbara Polo Grounds.

Santa Barbara Polo

El Fureidis

El Fureidis (*Little Paradise* or *Pleasure Gardens*) is a 10,000-square-foot historic estate built in 1906 on 10 acres in Montecito. Originally called the James Waldron Gillespie Estate or Gillespie Palace after its original owner, the Roman, Persian, Arabic, and Spanish-styled architecture is one of only five houses designed by the American architect Bertram Grosvenor Goodhue.

El Fureidis

The estate appeared in numerous hand-colored picture post cards from Santa Barbara during the 1900s–1950s highlighting Montecito's estates, the classical Persian gardens and Goodhue's unique architecture.

Stearns Wharf

Historic Stearns Wharf is California's oldest working wharf. When completed In 1872, it became the longest deep-water pier between Los Angeles and San Francisco. Named for its builder, local lumberman John P. Stearns, the wharf served the passenger and freight shipping needs of California's South Coast for over a quarter century.

Stearns Wharf

When the railroad reached Santa Barbara in 1877, Stearns added an additional spur to the wharf, providing a necessary transport link to his lumberyard and the nearby Southern Pacific Depot. The spur was damaged by severe storms in the early 20th century and was finally abandoned in 1923.

Santa Barbara Courthouse

The Courthouse has been called the most beautiful government building in America Designed by William Mooser III, the Spanish-Moorish style building was completed in 1929, after the 1925 earthquake ruined much of the city. It occupies a square block in downtown Santa Barbara. Gardens and lawns surround this working courthouse. Civic events, performances and numerous weddings are held on the attractively landscaped Sunken Garden where the 1872 courthouse once stood.

Santa Barbara Courthouse

Visitors can ride an elevator to the 85-foot "El Mirador" clock tower for unforgettable views of the city, coast and mountains. Other attractions include the Mural Room, "Spirit of the Ocean" fountain, noteworthy architecture and ornate tile work throughout the building.

Arlington Theater

Located at 1317 State Street, the Arlington was built in 1931 on the former site of the Arlington Hotel, which was destroyed following the 1925 earthquake. The current structure was erected in 1930 as a showcase movie house for Fox West Coast Theaters. It was restored and expanded in the mid-1970s by Metropolitan Theaters Corporation. It opened in its current incarnation in 1976.

Arlington Theater

The Arlington was designed in the Mission Revival and Spanish Colonial Revival styles in a period when Santa Barbara was being rebuilt in that style following a powerful earthquake in 1925. The exterior has a Mission Revival steeple that ends in an art deco finial. The red tiled building features a covered courtyard with fountain and a free-standing ticket booth.

The interior is elaborately decorated. The ceilings of the lobbies are heavily beamed and painted. The auditorium itself seats 2,000 on the main floor and balcony. It is built to give the theatergoer the impression that he is sitting outside in the plaza of a colonial Spanish town, each wall features houses, staircases, and balconies, not painted on but built out from the walls. The proscenium, in the original theater, was formed by what appeared to be a large stone arc, through which could be seen a river and hills (these were painted on the curtain.) Today, this effect is gone, and the proscenium is topped by the equipment necessary for lighting stage shows. The original ceiling remains to give patrons the impression that they are sitting outdoors under the stars.

Arlington Theater

One of the Arlington's signature features is a Robert Morton pipe organ hidden from view, that rises on a platform into view when played before a performance.

Mission Santa Barbara

Mission Santa Barbara, also known as Queen of the Missions, is a Spanish mission founded by the Franciscan order near present-day Santa Barbara. It was founded December 4, 1786, the feast day of Saint Barbara, as the tenth mission for the religious conversion of the indigenous local Chumash—Barbareño tribe of Native American people. The mission is the namesake of the city of Santa Barbara as well as Santa Barbara County.

Mission Santa Barbara

The Mission grounds occupy a rise between the Pacific Ocean and the Santa Ynez Mountains, and were consecrated by Father Fermín Lasuén, who had taken over the presidency of the California mission chain upon the death of Father Presidente Junípero Serra. Mission Santa Barbara is the only mission to remain under the leadership of the Franciscan Friars since its founding, and today is a parish church of the Archdiocese of Los Angeles.

Mission Santa Barbara's name comes from the legend of Saint Barbara, a girl who was supposedly beheaded by her father for following the Christian Faith. The early missionaries built three different chapels during the first few years, each larger than the previous one. It was only after the great Santa Barbara Earthquake on December 21, 1812, which destroyed the existing buildings, that the construction on the current Mission was begun. It was completed and then dedicated in 1820. The towers were considerably damaged in the June 29, 1925 earthquake, but were subsequently rebuilt in 1927. The appearance of the inside of the church has not been altered significantly since 1820.

The University of California, Santa Barbara

The University of California Santa Barbara, commonly known as UCSB or UC Santa Barbara, is a public research university and one of the 10 general campuses of the University of California system. The main campus is located on a 1,022-acre site in Goleta, 8 miles from Santa Barbara and 100 miles northwest of Los Angeles. Founded in 1891 as an independent teachers' college, UCSB joined the University of California system in 1944 and is the third-oldest general-education campus in the system.

University of California Santa Barbara

UCSB is a comprehensive doctoral university and is organized into five colleges offering 87 undergraduate degrees and 55 graduate degrees. The campus is the 5th-largest in the UC system by enrollment with 19,800 undergraduate and 3,050 graduate students. The university granted 5,442 bachelors, 576 masters, and 310 PhD degrees in 2006–2007. In 2012, UCSB was ranked 42nd among "National Universities" and 10th among public universities by U.S. News & World Report. The university was also ranked 29th worldwide by the Times Higher Education World University Rankings and 33rd worldwide by the Academic Ranking of World Universities in 2011.

UC Santa Barbara is a "very high activity" research university and spent $191.2 million on research expenditures in the 2007 fiscal year, 97th-largest in the United States. UCSB houses twelve national research centers, including the renowned Kavli Institute for Theoretical Physics. UCSB faculty includes five Nobel Prize laureates, one Fields Medalist, 29 members of the National Academy of Sciences, 27 members of the National Academy of Engineering, and 23 members of the American Academy of Arts and Sciences. UCSB was elected to the Association of American Universities in 1995. UCSB was the No. 3 host on the ARPAnet.

UCSB Lagoon

The UC Santa Barbara Gauchos compete in the NCAA Division I Big West Conference. The Gauchos have won NCAA national championships in men's soccer and men's water polo.

UCSB traces its origins back to the Anna Blake School which was founded in 1891 and offered training in home economics and industrial arts. The Anna Blake School was taken over by the state in 1909 and became the Santa Barbara State Normal School. In 1921, a liberal arts program was authorized and the school was renamed again to Santa Barbara State College. Intense lobbying by an interest group in the City of Santa Barbara, led by Thomas Storke and Pearl Chase, persuaded the State Legislature, Governor Earl Warren, and the Regents of the University of California to move the State College over to the more research-oriented University of California system in 1944. The State College system sued to stop the takeover, but the Governor did not support the suit. A state initiative was passed, however, to stop subsequent conversions of State Colleges to University of California campuses. From 1944 to 1958 the school was known as Santa Barbara College of the University of California, before taking on its current name.

UCSB Engineering

Originally, the Regents envisioned a small, several thousand-student liberal arts college, a so-called "Williams College of the West", at Santa Barbara. Chronologically, UCSB is the third general-education campus of the University of California after Berkeley and UCLA (the only other state campus to have been acquired by the UC system). The original campus the Regents acquired in Santa Barbara was located on only 100 acres of largely unusable land on a seaside mesa. The availability of a 400-acre portion of the land used as Marine Corps Air Station Santa Barbara until 1946 on another seaside mesa in Goleta, which the Regents could acquire for free from the federal government, led to that site becoming the Santa Barbara campus in 1949. Originally, only 3000–3500 students were anticipated, but the post WWII baby boom led to the designation of general campus in 1958, along with a name change from "Santa Barbara College" to "University of California, Santa Barbara," and the discontinuation of the industrial arts program for which the State college was famous. A Chancellor, Samuel B. Gould, was appointed in 1959. All of this change was done in accordance with the California Master Plan for Higher Education[5].

In 1959, UCSB Professor Douwe Stuurman hosted the English writer Aldous Huxley as the university's first visiting professor. Huxley delivered a lectures series called "The Human Situation".

In the late 1960s and early 1970s UCSB became nationally known as a hotbed of anti-Vietnam War activity. A bombing at the school's faculty club in 1969 killed the caretaker, Dover Sharp. In the spring 1970 multiple occasions of arson occurred, including a burning of the Bank of America branch building in the student community of Isla Vista, during which time one male student, Kevin Moran, was shot and killed by police. UCSB's anti-Vietnam activity impelled then Governor Ronald Reagan to impose a curfew and order the National Guard to enforce it. Weapon-carrying guardsmen were a common sight on campus and in Isla Vista during this time.

In 1995, UCSB was elected to the Association of American Universities, an organization of leading research universities, with a membership consisting of 59 universities in the United States (both public and private) and two universities in Canada.

---

[5] Editor's Note: Patricia Brown attended UCSB from 1961 until her graduation in 1965. She majored in Home Economics. She was one of the last to graduate from UCSB with that degree. The author attended UCSB from 1961 until his graduation, also in 1965. He majored in Electrical Engineering. He was a member of the first, ever, UCSB Engineering graduating class. In addition to academically bridging the old "Santa Barbara College" to the new "University of California at Santa Barbara" they lived through the initial explosive growth of the campus. Stident population grew from less than 4,000 to more than 10,000 in the couples four years there.

UCSB Santa Rosa Dormitory[6]

Santa Ynez Mountains

The Santa Ynez Mountains are a portion of the Transverse Ranges, part of the Pacific Coast Ranges of the west coast of North America and are one of the northernmost mountain ranges in Southern California. They are principally in Santa Barbara County, with an eastward extension into Ventura County, and are unusual in being an entirely east-west trending mountain range—one of the few in the United States.

---

[6] Editor's Note: Patricia Brown lived in the Santa Rosa dormitory from 1961 through the end of her junior year in 1964.

Santa Ynez Mountains

The mountains extend from an eastern terminus at the canyon of the Ventura River and Matilija Creek, north of Ojai, west across the Santa Barbara County line, to immediately north of the city of Santa Barbara, and then west, paralleling the coast, to the city of Lompoc and Vandenberg Air Force Base. The Santa Ynez River flows just north of the mountains, paralleling them for most of their length. Before reaching Lompoc the mountain range diverges into two low ranges, separated by Jalama Creek, which then vanish into the Pacific Ocean. The mountains parallel the Channel Islands to the south, another east-west trending range, a geologic extension of the Santa Monica Mountains; the two ranges are about thirty miles apart

Rancho del Cielo

Rancho del Cielo, or "Sky's or Heaven's Ranch," is a 688-acre ranch located on the top of the Santa Ynez Mountain range northwest of Santa Barbara. It served as a vacation home for President Ronald Reagan and First Lady Nancy Reagan.

Rancho del Cielo

The ranch was originally named Rancho de los Picos after José Jesús Pico, a descendant of Santiago de la Cruz Pico who came with the Anza expedition in 1776, who homesteaded it and built the original adobe house in 1871. The Reagans bought the ranch from in1974 when his second term as Governor of California was coming to an end. The estate contains a pond called Lake Lucky, stables and a barn for horses, and a 1,500 ft² house decorated with 1970s-style furniture. The ranch is located on the crest of the Santa Ynez Mountains adjacent to Refugio Pass. It can be reached from the ocean side of the mountains by the one-lane, paved Refugio Road from U.S. Route 101 (California 1), and from the other side of the mountains by an unpaved, one-lane road from Solvang . The dirt road may not be passable during the rainy season.

Reagan spent vacations during his presidency at the ranch, which became known as the Western White House. After leaving the presidency in 1989, the Reagans moved to a home in Bel-Air, but kept the ranch as a retreat. Ronald Reagan last visited the ranch in 1995 due to his affliction with Alzheimer's disease, and Mrs. Reagan last visited in 1998.

Point Conception

Point Conception is a headland located in southwestern Santa Barbara County. It is the point where the Santa Barbara Channel meets the Pacific Ocean, and as the corner between the mostly north-south trending portion of coast to the north and the east-west trending part of the coast near Santa Barbara, it makes a natural division between Southern and Central California. The Point Conception Lighthouse is at its tip.

Point Conception

Vandenberg Air Force Base

Vandenberg Air Force Base is a United States Air Force Base, located approximately 9.2 miles northwest of Lompoc. It is under the jurisdiction of the 30th Space Wing, Air Force Space Command.

Vandenberg AFB is a Department of Defense space and missile testing base, with a mission of placing satellites into polar orbit from the West Coast, using expendable boosters (Pegasus, Taurus, Minotaur, Atlas V and Delta IV). Wing personnel also support the Service's LGM-30G Minuteman III Intercontinental Ballistic Missile Force Development Evaluation program.

Vandenberg Air Force Base

The host unit at Vandenberg AFB is the 30th Space Wing. The 30th SW is home to the Western Range, manages Department of Defense space and missile testing, and places satellites into near-polar orbits from the West Coast. Wing personnel also support the Air Force's Minuteman III Intercontinental Ballistic Missile Force Development Test and Evaluation program. The Western Range begins at the coastal boundaries of Vandenberg and extends westward from the California coast to the Western Pacific, including sites in Hawaii. Operations involve dozens of federal and commercial interests.

Vandenberg Air Force Base

Vandenberg Air Force Base is named in honor of the late General Hoyt S. Vandenberg, second Air Force Chief of Staff of the United States Air Force and chief architect of today's modern Air Force. General Vandenberg was born in Milwaukee, Wisconsin, on January 24, 1899. In 1923, he graduated from West Point. During World War II, Colonel Vandenberg was transferred to England and assisted in planning air operations for the invasion of North Africa. He received his first star in December 1942, and became chief of staff of the Twelfth Air Force in North Africa under General James H. Doolittle. During this campaign he flew over two dozen combat missions over Tunisia, Italy, Sardinia, Sicily, and Panteileria to obtain firsthand information.

In March 1945, he was promoted to the rank of lieutenant general, and full general in 1947. Meanwhile, in January 1946, General Vandenberg was appointed chief of the intelligence division of the General Staff. In June, he was named director of the Central Intelligence Group, predecessor to the Central Intelligence Agency formed in 1947. With the establishment of a separate Air Force in September 1947, Vandenberg became its first vice chief of staff under General Carl Spaatz, and succeeded him on April 30, 1948. He held that post through the critical periods of the Berlin Airlift (1948–1949) and the Korean War (1950–1953).

Pismo Beach

Pismo Clams

Pismo Beach adopted the name "Clam Capital of the World" in the 1950s. The city holds the Clam Festival every October, complete with clam chowder competitions and a clam-themed parade. At the southern end of Price Street upon first entering Pismo Beach, a gigantic concrete clam statue greets visitors. Clamming once drew thousands of clammers to the beach during low tides and is still legal; however, due to over-harvesting by humans and the protected sea otter (which feasts on clams), few clams are to be found. An 8 inch shell of the Pismo clam (*Tivela stultorum*) is on display at the Pismo Beach Chamber of Commerce.

Pismo Beach

Pismo Beach Dunes are one of the few California beaches where it is legal to drive your vehicle on the sand. The family car can make a dash across the soft sand to the hard sand next to the water, but if you don't make it it's a very expensive tow out of the sand.

Motel Inn of San Luis Obispo

    Created in 1925 by Arthur Heineman, the Motel Inn of San Luis Obispo (originally known as the Milestone Mo-Tel) is the first motel in the world. It is located in San Luis Obispo.

    The emergence and popularization of the automobile in the United States of the early 20th century inspired many car owners beyond commuting into town. The poor roads of the era combined with the vehicle speeds and reliability required two or more days of nearly all day driving for 400-mile trips such as Los Angeles to San Francisco. Nearby destinations of 40 miles or less could be visited in a day to include a return trip. Longer trips requiring an over night stay often left travelers looking for places to pitch tent or to sleep in their automobile if arrangements hadn't been made ahead to destinations and stopovers that also happen to have hotels or inns.
The lack of niche accommodations to fill the need for automobile travelers who only needed an overnight stay to continue their trip inspired many entrepreneurs. The combination of the convenience of a campground with the comforts and respectability of a hotel or inn spurred the creation of the motel. Arthur S. Heineman picked San Luis Obispo for the first Milestone Mo-Tel as a mid-point location between Los Angeles and San Francisco which took two days of driving on the roads at the time.

Mo-Tel Inn

The original plan of the Milestone Mo-Tel was to include both bungalows and attached apartments with parking outside each unit, though some would have a private garage. Each location of the chain was to include laundry facilities, a grocery store, and a restaurant.
Each unit included an indoor bathroom with a shower, obviously a level of privacy not found at campgrounds. Heineman's first "Mo-Tel" sign garnered reports of an apparent misspelling. He added the hyphen to emphasize the compound nature of the word and the building's architecture and use. The exterior of the buildings were modeled after the Spanish missions in California; the three-stage bell tower was a reflection of the Mission Santa Barbara.

Moro Rock

Morro Rock is a 581-foot volcanic plug located just offshore from Morro Bay, at the entrance to Morro Bay Harbor. A causeway connects it with the shore, effectively making it a tied island. The area surrounding the base of Morro Rock can be visited. The rock is protected as the Morro Rock State Preserve. Climbing on the rock or disturbing the bird life is forbidden by law.

Moro Rock

Morro Rock was first charted in 1542 by Portuguese explorer Juan Rodriguez Cabrillo, who called it El Morro, the Spanish geographical term for a crown-shaped rock or hill ("the pebble"). Since then, it has become an important landmark to sailors and travelers.

Several types of birds nest on Morro Rock, including three cormorant species and two gull species. It presently serves as a reserve for peregrine falcons, which are locally endangered and cause most of the laws that prohibit intervention with avian life. Sea lions and sea otters can be seen regularly in the water around the rock. Seals, however, are much more common in the nearby Morro Bay State Park, where they breed.

Other fauna include a wide selection of tide pool animals, like hermit crabs, small fish, starfish, sea cucumbers, mussels, bivalve mollusks, coral, and more. On land few flora can survive the harsh, dry environment on the rock, but in the surrounding bay, kelp, sea grass, kelp forest plants, and tide pool plants can survive, and a few common grasses, mosses, lichens and weeds from the mainland take root on the rock itself.

Hearst Castle

Hearst Castle is a National Historic Landmark mansion located on the Central Coast, It was designed by architect Julia Morgan between 1919 and 1947 for newspaper magnate William Randolph Hearst, who died in 1951. In 1957, the Hearst Corporation donated the property to the state of California. Since that time it has been maintained as a state historic park where the estate, and its considerable collection of art and antiques, is open for public tours. Despite its location far from any urban center, the site attracts about one million visitors per year.

Hearst formally named the estate "La Cuesta Encantada" ("The Enchanted Hill"), but usually called it "the ranch". Hearst Castle and grounds are also sometimes referred to as "San Simeon" without distinguishing between the Hearst property and the adjacent unincorporated area of the same name.

Hearst Castle

Hearst Castle is located near the unincorporated community of San Simeon, approximately 250 miles from both Los Angeles and San Francisco, and 43 miles from San Luis Obispo at the northern end of San Luis Obispo County. The estate itself is five miles inland atop a hill of the Santa Lucia Range at an altitude of 1,600 feet. The region is sparsely populated because the Santa Lucia Range abuts the Pacific Ocean, which provides dramatic seaside vistas but few opportunities for development and hampered transportation. The surrounding countryside visible from the mansion remains largely undeveloped. Its entrance is adjacent to San Simeon State Park.

Hearst Castle was built on Rancho Piedra Blanca that William Randolph Hearst's father, George Hearst, originally purchased in 1865. The younger Hearst grew fond of this site over many childhood family camping trips. He inherited the ranch, which had grown to 250,000 acres and fourteen miles of coastline, from his mother Phoebe Hearst in 1919. Although the large ranch already had a Victorian mansion, the location selected for Hearst Castle was undeveloped, atop a steep hill whose ascent was a dirt path accessible only by foot or on horseback over five miles of cutbacks.

Hearst Castle

Hearst first approached American architect Julia Morgan with ideas for a new project in April 1915, shortly after he took ownership. Hearst's original idea was to build a bungalow, according to a draftsman who worked in Morgan's office who recounted Hearst's words from the initial meeting:

"I would like to build something upon the hill at San Simeon. I get tired of going up there and camping in tents. I'm getting a little too old for that. I'd like to get something that would be a little more comfortable."

After approximately one month of discussion, Hearst's original idea for a modest dwelling swelled to grand proportions. Discussion for the exterior style switched from an initial suggestion of Japanese and Korean themes to the Spanish

Revival that was gaining popularity and which Morgan had helped to initiate with her work on the *Los Angeles Herald Examiner* headquarters in 1915. Hearst was fond of Spanish Revival, but dissatisfied with the crudeness of the colonial structures in California Mexican colonial architecture had more sophistication but he objected to its profusion of ornamentation. Turning to the Iberian Peninsula for inspiration, he found Renaissance and Baroque examples in southern Spain more to his tastes. Hearst particularly admired a church in Ronda and asked Morgan to pattern the Main Building towers after it. The Panama-California Exposition of 1915 in San Diego held the closest approaches in California to the look Hearst desired. He decided to substitute a stucco exterior in place of masonry in deference to Californian traditions.

Hearst Castle

By late summer 1919 Morgan had surveyed the site, analyzed its geology, and drawn initial plans for the Main Building. Construction began in 1919 and continued through 1947 when Hearst stopped living at the estate due to ill health. Morgan persuaded Hearst to begin with the guest cottages because the smaller structures could be completed more quickly.

The estate is a pastiche of historic architectural styles that its owner admired in his travels around Europe. Hearst was a prolific buyer who did not so much purchase art and antiques to furnish his home as built his home to get his bulging collection out of warehouses. This led to incongruous elements such as the private cinema whose walls were lined with shelves of rare books. The floor plan of the Main Building is chaotic due to his habit of buying centuries-old ceilings, which dictated the proportions and decor of various rooms.

Hearst Castle

Hearst Castle featured 56 bedrooms, 61 bathrooms, 19 sitting rooms, 127 acres of gardens, indoor and outdoor swimming pools, tennis courts, a movie theater, an airfield, and the world's largest private zoo. Zebras and other exotic animals still roam the grounds. Morgan, an accomplished civil engineer, devised a gravity-based water delivery system which transports water from artesian wells on the slopes of Pine Mountain, a 3,500-foot high peak 7 miles east of Hearst Castle, to a reservoir on Rocky Butte, a 2,000-foot knoll less than a mile southeast from Hearst Castle.

One highlight of the estate is the outdoor Neptune Pool, located near the edge of the hilltop, which offers an expansive vista of the mountains, ocean and the main house. The Neptune Pool patio features an ancient Roman temple front, transported wholesale from Europe and reconstructed at the site. Hearst was an inveterate tinkerer, and would tear down structures and rebuild them at a whim. For example, the Neptune Pool was rebuilt three times before Hearst was satisfied. As a consequence of Hearst's persistent design changes, the estate was never completed in his lifetime.

Hearst Castle

Although Hearst Castle's ornamentation is borrowed from historic European themes, its underlying structure is primarily steel reinforced concrete. The use of modern engineering techniques reflects Morgan's background as a civil engineering graduate of the University of California, Berkeley and the first female architecture graduate of the École nationale supérieure des Beaux-Arts in Paris. During Hearst's ownership a private power plant supplied electricity to the remote location. Most of the estate's chandeliers have bare light bulbs, because electrical technology was so new when Hearst Castle was built.

Hearst Castle

Invitations to Hearst Castle were highly coveted during its heyday in the 1920s and '30s. The Hollywood and political elite often visited, usually flying into the estate's airfield or taking a private Hearst-owned train car from Los Angeles. Charlie Chaplin, Cary Grant, the Marx Brothers, Charles Lindbergh, Joan Crawford, Clark Gable, James Stewart, Bob Hope, Calvin Coolidge, Franklin Roosevelt, Dolores Del Rio, and Winston Churchill were among Hearst's A-list guests. While guests were expected to attend the formal dinners each evening, they were normally left to their own devices during the day while Hearst directed his business affairs. Since "the Ranch" had so many facilities, guests were rarely at a loss for things to do. The estate's theater usually screened films from Hearst's own movie studio, Cosmopolitan Productions.

Hearst Castle was the inspiration for the "Xanadu" mansion of the 1941 Orson Welles film *Citizen Kane*, which was itself a fictionalization of William Randolph Hearst's career. Hearst Castle itself was not used as a location for the film, which used Oheka Castle in New York.

One condition of the Hearst Corporation's donation of the estate was that the Hearst family would be allowed to use it when they wished. Patty Hearst, a granddaughter of William Randolph, related that as a child, she hid behind statues in the Neptune Pool while tours passed by. Although the main estate is now a museum, the Hearst family continues to use an older Victorian house on the property as a retreat — the original house built by George Hearst in the late 19th century. The house is screened from tourist routes by a dense grove of eucalyptus, to provide maximum privacy for the guests. In 2001, Patty Hearst hosted a Travel Channel show on the estate, and Amanda Hearst modeled for a fashion photo shoot at the estate for a Hearst Corporation magazine, *Town and Country*, in 2006.

Hearst Castle

Hearst Castle joined the National Register of Historic Places on June 22, 1972 and became a United States National Historic Landmark on May 11, 1976.

Big Sur Coast Highway

Follow Route One through the Big Sur area and take in the California coast the way it is meant to be experienced. From rocky embankments jutting into the clear blue waters of the Pacific to sea lions and other marine life playing in the coves and on the beaches, Big Sur is arguably the best way to appreciate the natural wonders of the western coast.

Big Sur

Big Sur is known for its peaceful atmosphere and tranquil setting. This makes it the perfect camping destination. Kirk Creek and Plasket Creek are two of the most beautiful spots on the entire coastline, and both are prime RV or tent camping locations. For those who want to get away from the road, Andrew Molera Campground offers hike-in campsites. Mild climate and diverse terrain make hiking in Big Sur another popular activity. Whether you are looking for an exciting outing for the family, an escape from the daily grind, or a romantic trip overlooking beautiful landscapes, you will find it while hiking Big Sur.

Big Sur

With views of rugged canyons and steep sea cliffs, granite shorelines and windswept cypress trees, majestic redwood forests and pristine coastline, you will feel the urge do nothing but sit back and relax. Find yourself rejuvenated by the warm breeze and romantic views. Play on the patches of sandy beach that dot the coastline, or swim in one of the secluded coves. Relax at a fine restaurant with a delicious meal, or picnic on one of the beaches. No matter what you choose to do in Big Sur, you will be sure to have a relaxing getaway that you will never forget.

Pebble Beach Golf Links

Pebble Beach is widely regarded as one of the most beautiful courses in the world. It hugs the rugged coastline and has wide open views of Carmel Bay, opening to the Pacific Ocean, on the south side of the Monterey Peninsula. In 2001 it became the first public course (i.e., open to the general public for play) to be selected as the No.1 Golf Course in America by *Golf Digest*. Greens fees are among the highest in the world.

Pebble Beach

There is no agreed upon "signature hole" at Pebble Beach Golf Links, but notable holes include the short par 3 7th, which plays to just over 100 yards even during major championships, is one of the most photographed holes in the world. From an elevated tee, players hit straight out toward the Pacific Ocean, with nothing in the background but the often violent Pacific Ocean surf crashing against rocky outcroppings. The long par 4 8th runs alongside the 6th hole leaving the peninsula and heading back toward the coastline. A dogleg right, the ocean is a constant companion along the entire right side of the hole. The landing area is extremely generous in width, but a long straight drive could leave the fairway and enter an inlet of the sea. Because the landing area is elevated on a cliff above the green, players have a good view of the small landing target a mid to long iron away. Jack Nicklaus has called this his favorite approach shot in all of golf.

Pebble Beach

Custom House

At one time, the Custom House presided over Mexico's primary port of entry on the Alta California coast. It was here that Commodore John Drake Sloat raised the American flag in July 1846, claiming over 600,000 square miles of territory for the United States. This territory later was included in all or portions of the states of Utah, Colorado, Arizona, California and New Mexico.

This building is recognized as the oldest government building in California. It is State Historic Landmark #1.

Custom House

Fisherman's Wharf

In 1769 Spaniard, Gaspar de Portola was sent north and in 1770 located Monterey Harbor and the ultimate City of Monterey was founded. California remained under Spanish control with Monterey as its capital until 1822, when Mexico added California to its empire. After war broke out between the United States and Mexico in 1846, Commodore Sloat, on landing in Monterey, claimed California for the Union.

Thus, the Marina, Old Fisherman's Wharf and Municipal Wharf II lie in some of the most historic waters in California.

Fisherman's Wharf

In 1870 the Pacific Coast Steamship Company constructed a wharf at Monterey for regular passenger and freight service, with ships arriving four times weekly. Growth of the sardine industry and the need to keep the Wharf in better repair prompted the City Council to assume ownership of the pier in 1913. (At some time during this period it became known as "Fisherman's Wharf")

By 1916 the City had purchased the Wharf and immediately began to expand the Wharf, providing more services to the fishing fleet and to the freight business. By 1920 the Wharf served as location for warehouses, nearly 20 wholesale and retail fish outlets, a marine service station, a restaurant, and an abalone shell grinding business.

On March 3, 1923, the largest load of sardines ever to be shipped from Monterey, 20,000 cases, was on Fisherman's Wharf ready to be loaded on the S.S. San Antonio. The weather was bad and the San Antonio leaned too heavily onto the Wharf timbers, causing 132 feet of the pier to collapse and spilling 10,000 cases of sardines into the harbor.

Fisherman's Wharf

Cannery Row, by John Steinbeck, takes place on a street lined with sardine fisheries in Monterey. It revolves around the people living there during the Great Depression: Lee Chong, the local grocer; Doc, a marine biologist based on Steinbeck's friend Ed Ricketts, and Mack, the leader of a group of bums.

Hang Gliding

Hang gliding is an air sport in which a pilot flies a light and unmotorized foot-launchable aircraft called a hang glider. Most modern hang gliders are made of an aluminium alloy or composite-framed fabric wing. The pilot is ensconced in a harness suspended from the airframe, and exercises control by shifting body weight in opposition to a control frame, but other devices, including modern aircraft flight control systems, may be used. In the sport's early days, pilots were restricted to gliding down small hills on low-performance hang gliders. However, modern technology gives pilots the ability to soar for hours, gain thousands of feet of altitude in thermal updrafts, perform aerobatics, and glide cross-country for hundreds of kilometres. The Fédération Aéronautique Internationale and national airspace governing organizations control some aspects of hang gliding. Seaside, on Monterey Bay, is a premier spot for hang gliding.

Hang Gliding at Seaside

SS Palo Alto

Seacliff is a California State Beach located off Highway 1 in the town of Aptos about 5 miles south of Santa Cruz, on State Park Drive. The beach's most notable feature is the concrete ship SS *Palo Alto* lying at the end of a pier. The ship was hauled to Seacliff Beach in 1929 and sank and turned into an amusement center complete with a dance floor, cafe, pool, and carnival booths. The Cal-Nevada Company constructed a dance floor on the main deck, a cafe in the superstructure of the ship, a 4-foot heated swimming pool and a series of carnival type concessions on the aft-deck. The Cal-Nevada Company went bankrupt after only two seasons and the ship was stripped. This left the pier and the ship used only for fishing[7].

SS Palo Alto

Santa Cruz

The present-day site of Santa Cruz was the location of Spanish settlement beginning in 1791, including Mission Santa Cruz and the *pueblo* of Branciforte. Following the Mexican–American War of 1846–48, California became the 31st state in 1850. The City of Santa Cruz was chartered in 1866. Important early industries included lumber, gunpowder, lime and agriculture. Late in the 19th century, Santa Cruz established itself as a beach resort community. Santa Cruz is now known for its moderate climate, the natural beauty of its coastline and redwood forests, alternative

---

[7] Editor's Note: For several years the author and his wife lived in a beach cottage very near the SS Palo Alto. The slowly settling concrete hull always added to the year-round beauty of the Monterey Bay.

community lifestyles, and socially liberal leanings. It is also home to the University of California, Santa Cruz, a premier research institution and educational hub, as well as the Santa Cruz Beach Boardwalk, an oceanfront amusement park.

Santa Cruz Boardwalk

The Giant Dipper is a historic wooden roller coaster located at the Santa Cruz Beach Boardwalk, an amusement park in Santa Cruz . It opened on May 17, 1924. It is the fifth-oldest roller coaster in the United States; over 55 million riders have ridden it since its opening. The United States National Park Service recognized the Giant Dipper as part of a National Historic Landmark in 1987.

As a center of liberal and progressive activism, Santa Cruz became one of the first cities to approve marijuana for medicinal uses. In 1992, residents overwhelmingly approved Measure A, which allowed for the medicinal uses of marijuana. Santa Cruz also became one of the first cities in California to test the state's medical marijuana laws in court after the arrest of Valerie Corral and Mike Corral, founders of the Wo/Men's Alliance for Medical Marijuana, by the DEA. The case was ruled in favor of the growers. In 2005, the Santa Cruz City Council established a city government office to assist residents with obtaining medical marijuana. On November 7, 2006, the voters of Santa Cruz passed Measure K by a vote of 64-36 percent. Measure K made adult non-medical cannabis offenses the lowest priority for law enforcement; this does not apply to cultivation, distribution, sale in public, sale to minors, or driving under the influence. The measure requests the Santa Cruz city clerk send letters annually to state and federal representatives advocating reform of cannabis laws.

Blue Whale

Robert "Wingnut" Weaver

The Surfer Interview

July 22, 2010

Robert "Wingnut" Weaver is a modern version of a Sixties Surfer. Or at least what we like to think of as a Sixties Surfer. With masterful flow, power and control, he is reminiscent of heroes like Phil Edwards, Mike Hynson and Mark Martinson. And it's a tribute to the man's style and soul that his unique, totally professional approach to having fun offers no contradiction. Because for Wingnut, it all seems to be about fun, a happy-go-lucky aura that belies all the hard work and dedication he's logged creating–with virtually no help at all from the mainstream surf media–one of the most enviable surf lifestyles in the business. With a grin and a good drop-knee cutback, he thrust into the limelight with a starring role in 1994's Endless Summer II. Flushed with success, Wingnut, now 37, parlayed the exposure into the kind of existence most of us–even other pros–could only dream about: a sponsored, traveling surfer and professional international surf guide for very affluent clientele. Then came a blunt twist of fate. In 1997, shortly after his son Cameron was born, Wingnut was diagnosed with multiple sclerosis, a degenerative disease of the nervous system that, among other things, affects one's balance and equilibrium. But characteristically irrepressible, Wingnut fought on. And hearing him tell about it is a reminder of how sweet life is. In his Santa Cruz home, just back from work in Surftech's marketing department, he sat down with his wife, Janice, son Cameron and beloved dog, Sheila, to spell it all out.

Robert "Wingnut" Weaver

SURFER: How did Wingnut get to be Wingnut? We won't even ask about the nickname.

WINGNUT: My family moved from Cologne, Germany, to Newport Beach back in the 1970s and I basically grew up right in front of Blackies riding longboards, watching classic Newport guys like Don Craig. From that I developed an affinity for what I like to call "classical" longboarding. I did the longboard contest circuit in the late 80s and early 90s, but it was never a good fit. The club contests were fun, and I was winning. I won Oceanside and I won at Malibu…I was right there, poised for God knows what, because there was no money in it. I was competing against any and all of the 25 different Paskowitz brothers and sisters and then came Joel. Joel was like 14, and if he kept his head about him, he could've won anything he wanted to. But he was still flustered. It was funny, because you'd have Donald Takayama or David Nuuhiwa on the beach with Joel's mom and dad and they'd all be yelling separate instructions to this poor little kid who could surf better than all of them. I especially remember the Malibu contest because Joel finally just stood up on his board, tears streaming down his face, yelling back at them to all shut up. Seeing the state he was in, I pressed my advantage and won the event. Still, I knew competing exclusively just wasn't for me.

SURFER: If not the traditional path of a surfer who wants to make it his living, then what?

WINGNUT: Well, then what happened was Endless Summer II. There was life before, then life after the movie.

SURFER: How did it happen?

WINGNUT: Well, I graduated in 1991 from UC Santa Cruz with a degree in economics and marketing. So at that point, as a longboarder, there was no real way to make money surfing competitively. I mean, O'Neill was giving me wetsuits and I was getting free boards, so at least my hobby was free. The club contests were fun, you know, it's all about the barbecue, but making a living? I think back to a low moment when I was at one Oceanside contest. It was Friday at dawn and I already lost my heat. In an announcer's voice: "How bout a hand for Wingnut, all the way from Santa Cruz. Great to see you; see you next time…the beer garden will be open at noon."
Something had to be done. So I graduated, Janice and I got married that October, came back from honeymoon and said, "What now?"

SURFER: How did you pay rent?

WINGNUT: Waiting tables down at the Crow's Nest, like all good little surfers. The only thing I was sure of was I wanted to make surfing my life. So my plan was to save up and go down to the January Action Sport's Retailer trade show in San Diego to get a job. I wanted to work in the industry. Then it happened. It was January 14th, 1992 at 1:15 in the afternoon. The phone rang and it was Bruce Brown. Impersonating Bruce Brown: "Yeah, uh, Wingnut? Yeah this is Bruce Brown and we're gonna be doing a sequel to Endless Summer and were wondering if you would want to be one of the guys." So I said, "Well, gee, I don't know, I gotta mow the lawn and do some laundry but if I hurry I think I can make it down there by three." Bruce got a kick out of that. So I went and saw him on the way to the trade show and he told me I had the job. And that's what allowed me to get out of the dead-end competition scene. The movie contract was a two-year, 24-hour notice deal. And Bruce allowed me to negotiate my own contracts within the surf industry.

SURFER: A surfer's version of hitting the lottery.

Natural Bridges State Beach

Natural Bridges State Beach is a 65-acre California state park in Santa Cruz, in the United States. The park features a natural bridge across a section of the beach. It is also well known as a hotspot to see monarch butterfly migrations. The Monarch Butterfly Natural Preserve is home to up to 150,000 monarch butterflies from October through early February.

Monarch Butterflies

    Natural Bridges State Beach is home to a eucalyptus grove that provided habitat for monarch butterflies. Up to 150,000 butterflies migrate up to 2,000 miles to the park to escape the cold weather of winter in the northwestern United States and Canada. The city of Santa Cruz holds an annual festival to mark the return of the butterflies. Monarchs settle in groves along the coasts of California and Baja California. At Natural Bridges State Beach they find shelter from the wind and sources of water and food. The butterflies cluster onto the trees, "intertwining their legs among the branches to resemble a clump of leaves." The butterflies protect each other from cold winter winds and rains by clustering together. Beginning in the late 1990s the population of butterflies at the park began to decline. Biologist attribute the decline to a lack of habitat caused by fallen pine and eucalyptus trees. The decline at Natural Bridges State Beach has meant an increase in butterfly numbers at nearby Lighthouse Field State Beach.

Section 5

Half Moon Bay to Eureka

California 1 to US 101

Maverick's

Maverick's is a surfing location in Northern California. It is located approximately 2 miles from shore in Pillar Point Harbor just north of Half Moon Bay at the village of Princeton-By-The-Sea. After a strong winter storm in the northern Pacific Ocean, waves can routinely crest at over 25 feet and top out at over 80 feet.

Mavericks is a winter destination for some of the world's best big wave surfers. Very few riders become big wave surfers; and of those, only a select few are willing to risk the hazardous conditions at Maverick's. An invitation-only contest is held there every winter, depending on wave conditions.

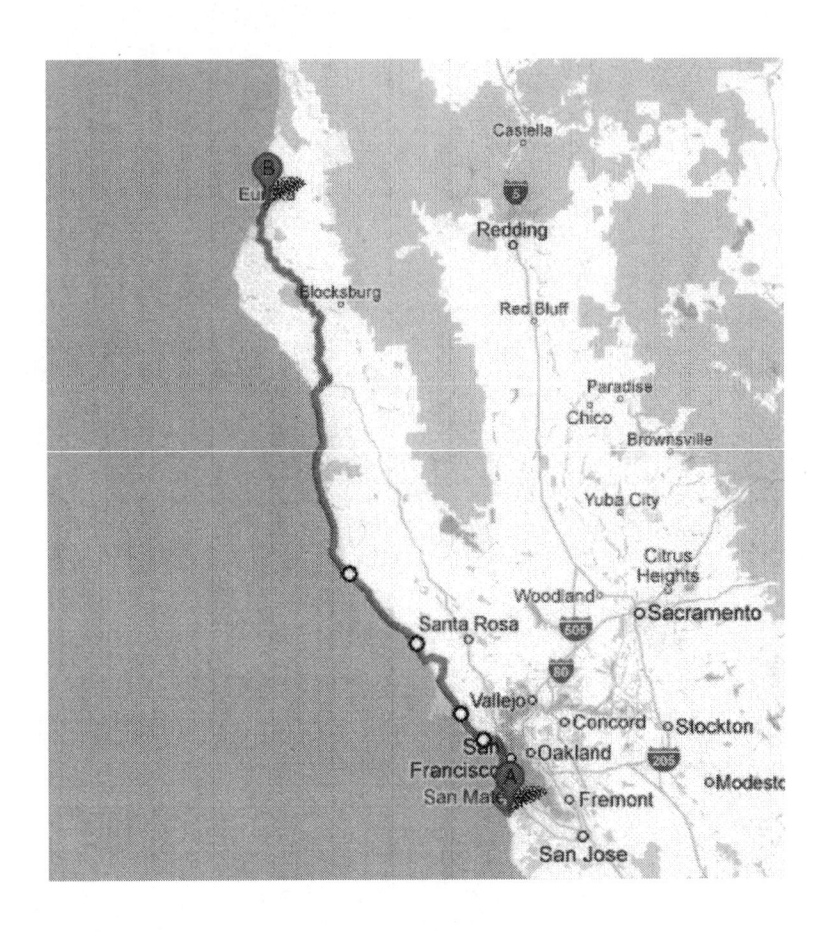

Half Moon Bay to Eureka (Google Maps)

Maverick's

Sea-floor maps released by the US National Oceanic and Atmospheric Administration in 2007 revealed why Mavericks' waves form where they do. A long, sloping ramp leads up to the surface under the wavebreak. The presence of this ramp slows the propagation of the wave over it. The wave over the deep water troughs on each side of the ramp continues at full speed forming two angles in the wavefront centered over each of the boundaries between the ramp and the two troughs. The result of this is a U-shaped or V-shaped wavefront on the ramp that contains the wave energy from the full width of the ramp. This U-shaped or V-shaped wave then collapses into a small area at the top center of the ramp with tremendous force.

Devil's Slide

Devil's Slide is a name given to a steep, rocky coastal promontory located about midway between Montara and the Linda Mar District of Pacifica. The terrain is characterized by steep, eroded slopes with natural gradients ranging between 30 and

70%. There are small coastal valleys throughout along the major drainages within the Montara Mountain watershed. The soils in these valleys are deep and moderately well drained and have developed along the low terraces and alluvial fans of the stream channels.

Immediately north of Devil's Slide is a stretch of California's State Route 1, famous for closures and landslides, which is also called "Devil's Slide". Construction of the road began in 1935 and was completed in 1937, replacing the steep, narrow, and winding Pedro Mountain Road. It is known for the landslides and erosion that often occur during winter storms, sometimes making the road impassable. The first major landslide destroyed much of the road in 1940, and a cycle of building and destruction has prevailed since.

Devil's Slide

Golden Gate Park

Golden Gate Park, located in San Francisco, is a large urban park consisting of 1,017 acres of public grounds. Configured as a rectangle, it is similar in shape but 20% larger than Central Park in New York, to which it is often compared. It is over three miles long east to west, and about half a mile north to south. With 13 million visitors annually, Golden Gate is the third most visited city park in the United States after Central Park in New York City and Lincoln Park in Chicago.

Golden Gate Park

In the 1860s, San Franciscans began to feel the need for a spacious public park similar to Central Park that was taking shape in New York. Golden Gate Park was carved out of unpromising sand and shore dunes that were known as the "outside lands" in an unincorporated area west of then-San Francisco's borders. Although the park was conceived under the guise of recreation, the underlying justification was to attract housing development and provide for the westward expansion of The City. The tireless field engineer William Hammond Hall prepared a survey and topographic map of the park site in 1870 and became commissioner in 1871. He was later named

California's first State Engineer and developed an integrated flood control system for the Sacramento Valley when he was not working on Golden Gate Park.

Golden Gate Park

    The actual plan and planting were developed by Hall and his assistant, John McLaren, who had apprenticed in Scotland, the homeland of many of the 19th century's best professional gardeners. The initial plan called for grade separations of transverse roadways through the park, as Frederick Law Olmsted had provided for Central Park, but budget constraints and the positioning of the Arboretum and the Concourse ended the plan. In 1876, the plan was almost exchanged for a racetrack favored by "the Big Four" millionaires, Leland Stanford, Mark Hopkins, Collis P. Huntington, and Charles Crocker. Hall resigned and the remaining park commissioners followed him. The original plan, however, was back on track by 1886, when streetcars delivered over 47,000 people to Golden Gate Park on one weekend afternoon (the city's population at the time was about 250,000). Hall selected McLaren as his successor in 1887.

Golden Gate Park

     The first stage of the park's development centered on planting trees, in order to stabilize the ocean dunes that covered three-quarters of the park's area. By 1875, about 60,000 trees, mostly Blue Gum Eucalyptus, Monterey pine and Monterey cypress, had been planted. By 1879, that figure had more than doubled to 155,000 trees over 1,000 acres. Later McLaren scoured the world through his correspondents for trees. When McLaren refused to retire at age 60, as was customary, the San Francisco city government was bombarded with letters: when he reached 70, a charter amendment was passed to exempt him from forced retirement. He lived in McLaren Lodge in Golden Gate Park until he died at age 96, in 1943.

Golden Gate Park

In 1903, a pair of Dutch-style windmills were built at the extreme western end of the park. These pumped water throughout the park. The north windmill has been restored to its original appearance and is adjacent to a flower garden, a gift of Queen Wilhelmina of the Netherlands. These are planted with tulip bulbs for winter display and other flowers in appropriate seasons. The Murphy Windmill in the southwest corner of the park was recently restored.

Most of the water used for landscape watering and for various water features is now provided by groundwater from the City's Westside Basin Aquifer. However, the use of highly processed and recycled effluent from the city's sewage treatment plant, located at the beach some miles away to the south near the San Francisco Zoo is planned for the near future. In the 1950s the use of this effluent during cold weather caused some consternation, with the introduction of artificial detergents but before the advent of modern biodegradable products. These "hard" detergents would cause long-lasting billowing piles of foam to form on the creeks connecting the artificial lakes and could even be blown onto the roads, forming a traffic hazard.

Golden Gate Park

Golden Gate Park is adjacent to Haight-Ashbury, and it was the site of the Human Be-In of 1967, preceding the Summer of Love. The tradition of large, free public gatherings in the park continues to the present, especially at Hellman Hollow. Originally named Speedway Meadow, it was renamed in 2011 in honor of Warren Hellman. In 2001, Hellman founded the Hardly Strictly Bluegrass Festival (formerly the "Strictly Bluegrass Festival"), a free music festival held in October. Hellman Hollow also plays host to a number of large-scale events such as the 911 Power to the Peaceful Festival held by musician and filmmaker Michael Franti.

Since the 1980s, the city of San Francisco has grappled with what to do about large encampments of chronically-homeless people living in Golden Gate Park, which have been criticized as unsanitary, unsafe and "demoralizing" for park users and workers. The camps have been described by journalists as full of garbage, broken glass, hypodermic needles and human excrement, and the people in them are described as chronically homeless, many suffering from serious addictions, and often behaving aggressively with police and park gardeners. There have been occasional incidents of violence and vandalism related to the homeless in the park, including the 2010 park beating to death of a homeless man and an attack on park visitors by dogs owned by a park resident, also in 2010.

San Francisco Cable Cars

The San Francisco cable car system is the world's last manually operated cable car system. An icon of San Francisco, the cable car system forms part of the intermodal urban transport network operated by the San Francisco Municipal Railway, or "Muni" as it is better known. Of the twenty-three lines established between 1873 and 1890, three remain (one of which combines parts of two earlier lines): two routes from downtown near Union Square to Fisherman's Wharf, and a third route along California Street. While the cable cars are used to a certain extent by commuters, their small service area and premium fares for single rides make them more of a tourist attraction. The cable cars are the only mobile National Monument.

Single-ended cars serve the Powell-Hyde and Powell-Mason lines. These cars have an open-sided front section, with outward-facing seats flanking the gripman and a collection of levers that actuate the grip and various brakes. The rear half of the car is enclosed, with seats facing inward and entrances at each end and the car has a small platform at the rear. Double-ended cars serve the California Street line. These cars are somewhat longer, having open-sided grip sections at both ends and an enclosed section in the middle. Both types of car ride on a pair of four-wheel trucks, to fit the track gauge of 3 ft 6 in.

Cable Car

The driver of a cable car is known as the *gripman* or grip person. This is a highly skilled job, requiring the gripman to smoothly operate the grip lever to grip and release the cable, release the grip at certain points to coast the vehicle over crossing cables or places where the cable does not follow the tracks, and to anticipate well in advance possible collisions with other traffic that may not understand the limitations of a cable car. Being a gripman requires great upper body strength needed for the grip and brakes, as well as good hand-eye coordination and balance. On the second or third Thursday each July, a cable car bell-ringing contest is held in Union Square between cable car crews, following a preliminary round held during the second to last or the last week of June.

Cable Car Turn-Around

Emperor Norton

Peter Moylan

San Francisco Museum and Historical Society

To today's San Franciscan, the name "Emperor Norton" conjures up images of a colorful, but homeless street person, accompanied by a couple of dogs, who ordered bridges to be built and governments dissolved; an insane man revered by the San Franciscans of the late 19th Century. His story is far more complex than most San Franciscans know.

The real Emperor - Joshua Abraham Norton - is one of contradictions and myths. He was rational man who could speak about any intelligently about politics and science, was a great chess player, and was quite inventive, but believed he was the Emperor of the United States and Protector of Mexico. He issued proclamations, collected taxes, attended sessions of government, rode free on public transit, had free tickets to theater, and sold his own currency; but lived day to day as a pauper in raggedy clothes. He was a successful businessman who lost a fortune as the result of a business deal gone badly and ultimately lived off the kindness of San Franciscans, but owned no dogs and was never homeless.

Emperor Norton

The contradictions start at his very birth. There is a record of the birth of a Joshua Norton to a John and Sarah Norton in Priorslee (now Telford), Shropshire, England (147 miles northwest of London) on January 17, 1811. However, Norton is a common surname in England.

In 1820, John and Sarah Norton and their three children were among a handful of Jews emigrating with 5,000 British to Algoa Bay, South Africa. John Norton was a leader of the Jewish community. They were called the 1820 Settlers and were instrumental in the creation of Port Elizabeth in South Africa. Norton's biographer, William Drury, wrote that John Norton told immigration officials that Joshua was 2, which would have placed his birth in 1818. Others claim he was born in February of 1819, but no evidence supports that date. Based on events in his later life, it seems that 1818 is the most likely year of his birth.

In 1841, the family moved to Cape Town, South Africa. Norton started his own business, but in 18 months was bankrupt. He went to work as a clerk in his father's ship chandlery. By 1848, his mother, and two brothers, and father had died. To Joshua went his father's estate, worth about $40,000.

In 1849, Norton was lured, as hundreds of thousands would be, to San Francisco by the dream of fortunes to be made in the Gold Rush. Norton did not seek his fortune in the hard gold fields of the Sierra Nevada foothills; instead he would try to make his fortune in real estate and business. He signed into the William Tell House as Joshua Abraham Norton, international merchant.

Joshua Norton, San Francisco and the Gold Rush

Joshua Norton & Company, General Merchants, was founded in a cottage made of adobe bricks at Jackson and Montgomery Streets, which Norton rented from a miserly old man named James Lick. He bought a ship anchored in the Yerba Buena Cove, the Genessee, to store his own merchandise and rent space to others for storage, a common use for ships abandoned in San Francisco by crews headed to the gold fields.

In 1851, his adobe cottage burned in a major fire. Norton relocated to a substantial granite building at 110 Battery Street, which housed the offices of several of influential people, including the British Consul. He hobnobbed with San Francisco's business and social elite. He was a charter member of the Occidental Lodge #22 of the Freemasons.

He acquired parcels on three corners of Sansome and Jackson Streets, on which he opened a cigar factory, a small wood-framed office building, and a rice mill. He purchased a few lots by Rincon Point, where the value increased dramatically when the Pacific Mail Steamship Company built a passenger terminal and warehouse nearby. And he bought several lots that were to be developed by Harry Meiggs on North Beach.

Norton's World Collapses

By 1852, Norton's assets were estimated at $250,000, about $5 million today, and he saw the opportunity for more. China was the main supplier of rice to California until a famine cut off shipments. Scarcity drove the price from four cents per pound to 36 cents. At the Merchant's Exchange, where commodities were bought, sold and traded, the mercantile bank Goddefroy and Sillem was agent for the Ruiz Brothers, who owned a ship called *The Glyde*, in the harbor with 200,000 pounds of rice from Peru. Willy Sillem pulled Norton aside, showed him a handful and told him he could buy it all and corner the rice market for only 12½ cents a pound, or $25,000 for the whole shipload. At 36 cents a pound, he could gross $72,000, nearly a 200% profit.

On December 22, 1852, he put $2,000 down, with a contract to pay it all in 30 days. The next day, a ship full of Peruvian rice sailed into San Francisco, followed by several more ships in less than two weeks. The rice on these ships was of far superior quality to that on the Glyde. The price of rice crashed to three cents a pound. Norton tried to nullify the contract on the grounds that he was misled by Willy Sillem - the rice on *The Glyde* was inferior to the sample shown him. The Glyde's owners sued Norton for payment of the $23,000 due. For the next 2½ years, they battled in court, racking up enormous legal bills. In 1855, the court ruled for *The Glyde's* owners.

And now, the gold rush was over - the flow of gold dust had become a trickle. There was glut of everything in San Francisco; prices crashed, cargoes rotted on the wharves; the real estate market collapsed, businesses were closing, banks were failing, bankruptcy was common. San Francisco herself was near ruin. And so was Norton.

The bank foreclosed on his North Beach and Fisherman's Wharf properties. He had to sell his businesses and properties on Sansome and Jackson at a huge loss. Then he was accused of embezzling funds from a client. All he had left was his Rincon Point properties to use as collateral for a loan to settle the matter.

He was no longer invited to the parties of the social and business elite. His membership in the Freemasons was cancelled for failure to pay dues. He went from living in the finest hotels to run-down boarding houses of the working class.

On August 25, 1856, a brief notice appeared in the *Bulletin* newspaper - "Joshua Norton, filed a petition for the benefit of the Insolvency Law. Liabilities $55,811; assets stated at $15,000, uncertain value." In 1857 and 1858, his name appeared on occasion in the *Daily Alta* in advertisements as a "commission agent," brokering sales of barley, coffee and linseed oil. The City Directory showed that by 1858, he was living at 255 Kearny, a boarding house of the working class that would not have been the home of the successful businessman.

The Birth of an Emperor

19th Century Americans saw their nation as a burgeoning empire, reflected in San Francisco by the Empire House Hotel, Empire Saloon, Empire Brewery, Empire Oil Works, and the Empire Fire Engine Company #1.

But to Norton, America's Republican form of government was one of inefficiency, corruption, self-interest. How could America be an empire if its leaders were elected? He admired the English monarchy; the British Empire. In 1852, he had casually remarked to a friend: "If I were Emperor of the United States, you would see great changes effected, and everything would go harmoniously."

In 1859, everything was not going harmoniously. California was caught up in the great debate over slavery that would lead to the nation's darkest hour - the Civil War. In a fiery speech in Sacramento attacking abolitionists, California State Supreme Court Justice David S. Terry denounced and ridiculed United States Senator David C. Broderick, political boss of San Francisco. Broderick was outraged, and called Terry "the damned miserable wretch," which outraged Terry. In California's last formal duel, Terry shot Broderick dead.

On September 17, 1859, climbed the stairs of 517 Clay Street to the office of the *San Francisco Bulletin* newspaper. George Fitch, editor of the Bulletin, was sitting at his desk when a man he described as "neatly dressed and serious looking" handed him a piece of paper. The next morning, Fitch ran a headline: "Have We An Emperor Among Us?" and printed the following proclamation.

"At the pre-emptory request of a large majority of the citizens of these United States, I Joshua Norton, formerly of Algoa Bay, Cape of Good Hope, and now for the last nine years and ten months past of San Francisco, California declare and proclaim myself the Emperor of These United States, and in virtue of the authority thereby in me vested do hereby order and direct the representatives of the different States of the Union to assemble in Musical Hall of this city, on the 1st day of February next, then and there to make such alterations in the existing laws of the Union as may ameliorate the evils under which the country is laboring, and thereby cause confidence to exist, both at home and abroad, in our stability and integrity."

It was signed: "Norton I, Emperor of the United States."

The Emperor's Reign Begins

But in San Francisco, the reign of Emperor Norton I was to begin. Less than a month later, on October 12, the *Bulletin* published his next proclamation under an excited headline: "Another Ukase from Czar Norton - Congress Abolished. Take notice, the world! His Imperial Majesty, Norton I, has issued the following edict, which he desires the *Bulletin* to spread to the world. Let her rip."

"It is represented to us that the universal suffrage, as now existing throughout the Union, is abused; that fraud and corruption prevent a fair and proper expression of the public voice; that open violation of the laws are constantly occurring, caused by mobs, parties, factions and undue influence of political sects; that the citizen has not that protection of person and property which he is entitled to by paying his pro rata of the expense of government - in consequence of which, WE do hereby abolish congress, and it is therefore abolished; and We order and desire the representatives of all parties interested to appear at the Musical Hall of this city on the first of February next, and then and there take the most effective steps to remedy the evil complained of."

Two weeks later, Norton abolished the California Supreme Court for a perceived slight to His Majesty.

Norton then learned Virginia governor Henry A. Wise had sent radical abolitionist John Brown to the gallows for his attack on the federal arsenal at Harper's Ferry. Norton didn't approve of Brown's actions, but stated: "the said Brown was insane and that he ought to have been sent to the Insane Asylum for capturing the State of Virginia with seventeen men." So, Norton Fired Governor Wise and replaced him with John C. Breckinridge of Kentucky, who was otherwise occupied with the job of Vice President of the United States.

In the first week of 1860, Congress convened in Washington in clear violation of Norton's edict of October 12. Norton ordered General Winfield Scott, "Commander-in-Chief of the Armies ... to clear the hall of Congress." General Scott had been Commander of the Armies 15 years earlier in the Mexican American War. He was now 74, and was not in Washington D.C., but in the Washington Territory, negotiating with Canada over ownership of islands off the coast near the border.

Having twice called for a meeting on February 1 "of the interested parties" at Platt's Music Hall, Norton was frustrated when the hall burned to the ground just a few days earlier. Norton rescheduled the meeting for February 5 at the Assembly Hall, at Kearny and Post Streets. The Bulletin, sensing a great story, urged folks to get there early for a good seat. Perhaps seriously, perhaps in jest, the Bulletin wrote: "take a chair, a blanket or two, an umbrella, a pile of sandwiches, a bottle of something ... be ready, when the time comes, for the squeeze. Wednesday is going to be a great day for California." But when Emperor Norton arrived at the Assembly Hall, the doors were locked; the hall dark; nary a soul was there.

The *Bulletin* did publish Norton's entire prepared speech, talking about the problems that faced the nation, part of which said: "Taking all of these circumstances into consideration, and the internal dissensions on Slavery, we are certain that nothing will save the nation from utter ruin except an absolute monarchy under the supervision and authority of an independent Emperor."

In July 1860, Norton ordered the Republic of the United States to be dissolved for an "Absolute Monarchy." His proclamation read:

"We are certain that nothing will save the nation from utter ruin except an absolute monarchy under the supervision and authority of an independent Emperor."

In 1869, he abolished the Democratic and Republican parties. King George III would have been proud.

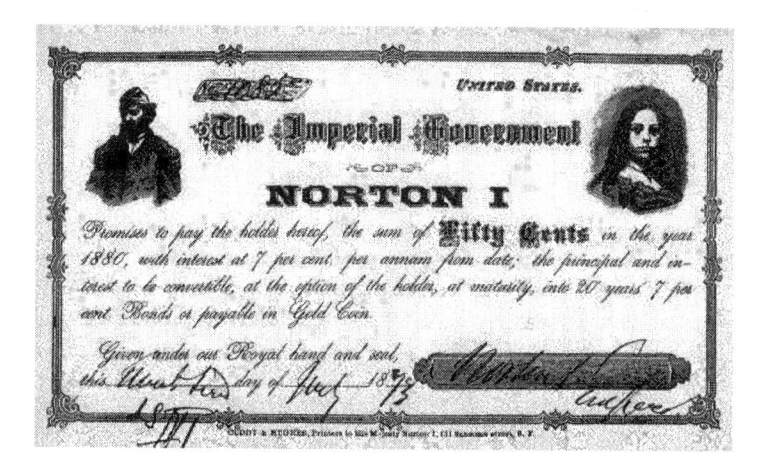

Norton 50 Cent Script

As early as 1861, Norton's legend was growing. Norton the First, a play, debuted on a San Francisco stage. While he probably would not have wanted to attend that play, one of the best seats at the theaters was always reserved on opening night for Norton. Playgoers applauded and the orchestra played a fanfare upon his arrival, escorted to his seat by the manager.

203

When Napoleon III, nephew of the first Napoleon, invaded Mexico in 1863, the Emperor added a new title: "Protector of Mexico." There is no evidence Norton ever stepped foot in Mexico.

Politicians courted him; to show him disrespect would be to lose votes. In 1867, policeman Armand Barbier made the mistake of arresting Norton for vagrancy. The desk sergeant pointed out that Norton had $4.75 and a key to his room at the Eureka Lodgings in his pockets. To save face, Barbier charged Norton with lunacy.

Under a picture of Norton in his full uniform, the Evening Bulletin wrote: "In what can only be described as the most dastardly of errors, Joshua A. Norton was arrested today. He is being held on the ludicrous charge of 'Lunacy.' Known and loved by all true San Franciscan's as Emperor Norton, this kindly Monarch of Montgomery Street is less a lunatic than those who have engineered these trumped up charges. As they will learn, His Majesty's loyal subjects are fully apprised of this outrage. Perhaps a return to the methods of the Vigilance Committees is in order.

"This newspaper urges all right-thinking citizens to be in attendance tomorrow at the public hearing to be held before the Commissioner of Lunacy, Wingate Jones. The blot on the record of San Francisco must be removed."

The Alta wrote: "The Emperor Norton has never shed blood. He has robbed no one, and despoiled no country. And that, gentlemen, is a hell of a lot more than can be said for anyone else in the king line."

Police Chief Patrick Crowley released Norton, with his apology, and from then all police officers would salute Norton when he passed them on the street.

The Newspapers Role in Creating the Emperor

While the *Bulletin* stayed true to Norton's actual proclamations, The *Daily Alta California* quickly realized a potential bonanza. Unlike today, most cities had several fiercely competitive newspapers - San Francisco had at least five. Anything that made a good story sold papers and Norton was the quintessential good story.

Albert Evans, editor of the *Alta*, quickly realized a potential bonanza. Known as Colonel Mustache for his flamboyant facial hair, Evans began printing phony proclamations, some clever, some silly, attributed to Norton, designed to generate laughs or ridicule. They were written in a style clearly lacking Norton's precision and logic. Others occasionally fooled the editors with proclamations presumed to be from Norton to push political or other points of view.

One writer who sympathized with the Emperor was a reporter for the *Daily Morning Call* named Samuel Langhorne Clemens, later to be known by the name Mark Twain. Twain would from time to time include Emperor Norton in his column. He wrote of Norton: "O dear, it was always a painful thing for me to see the Emperor begging, for although nobody else believed he was an emperor, he believed it."

Reporters learned very quickly that associating Emperor Norton with a restaurant or a clothing store would generate free publicity for the merchant and free food and clothing for the reporter. And businesses quickly learned that a bribe to the editors could also get you some publicity if Emperor Norton was involved. One haberdasher gave Norton an old hat that was no longer in style so he could advertise in the papers: "Gentleman's Outfitters to His Imperial Majesty." Restaurants claimed Emperor Norton as a patron. A tavern posted a window sign that said "Fine wines and spirituous liquors by Appointment to his Majesty, Norton I." Rarely did the generosity extend beyond a single instance.

The Real Life of the Emperor

In reality, Norton was now living off the kindness of his former business acquaintances and Freemasons. He was bone thin, with raggedy clothes. Norton would take their help of the occasional 50 cent piece for lunch or rent, but to save face, he simply referred to it as a tax, and recorded his tax collections in a notebook. He then began to visit local businesses, as often as monthly, to collect taxes, which some gave out of fondness for the Emperor.

Unlike a certain fabled emperor, this Emperor had clothes - but these were hardly the clothes of an emperor. He wore all manner of well-worn uniforms given to him by the Army at the Presidio or purchased from the auction houses along Pacific

Street on the old Barbary Coast. On informal occasions Norton would wear a soft hat called a kepi and a coat of either blue or grey; he was after all, the Emperor of all the States.

For formal occasions, he had built himself an outfit of a stained and worn a Union officer's coat, enhanced with epaulets of tarnished gold and a boutonniere in the lapel, a tall beaver hat adorned with ostrich plume, a cavalry sword on his hip and an twisted knotty wood walking stick with ornate handle and a silver plate engraved Norton I, Emperor U.S. When it rained, he carried a tri-colored Chinese umbrella.

In 1863, Norton took a room in the Eureka Lodgings, a flophouse at 624 Commercial Street, between Montgomery and Kearny. He paid 50 cents a night for the next 17 years. His room was nine-feet by six-feet, with an iron cot with rickety springs, a chair, a sagging couch with soiled upholstering, a washbasin, and a night table. There was no closet. He hung his clothes on "ten-penny" nails in the wall. Logically, he was attracted to royalty. Lithographs of Queen Victoria of England, Queen Emma of the Sandwich Islands (now Hawaii), Empress Carlotta of Mexico, and Empress Eugenie, the wife of Napoleon the III graced his squalid walls.

The official United States Census taker in 1870 recorded the presence of Norton. In the column marked occupation was the entry: "emperor." In the column that explained why Norton was not eligible to vote, the census taker chose the option of "insane."

His days followed a regular pattern. He would dress in his uniform, pay the daily rent, and walk next door to the fancy Empire House hotel to read the newspapers. He then walked a block and a half to Portsmouth Square, where he would spend the afternoons on park benches with his friends. "He carried a dignified and regal air about him, but was seen as a kind, affable man, inclined to be jocular in conversation. He spoke rationally and intelligently about any subject, except about himself or his empire," wrote his biographer, William Drury.

In Norton's day, it was rare for a Chinese person to be in Portsmouth Square, but one of Norton's constant companions was Ah How. The Daily Alta called him Norton's Grand Chamberlain. Norton abhorred the treatment of Chinese, decrying the immigration laws that denied entry to a man because of the color of his skin. He demanded that the laws prohibiting Chinese from testifying in court be repealed. When a mob threatened a few Chinese, he broke through the crowd, spoke the Lord's Prayer and said "we are all God's children."

When Old St. Mary's church bells signaled noon, Norton headed to Martin & Horton's on Clay near Montgomery or the Bank Exchange for his "free" lunch, which anyone could have for the price of a drink. Norton didn't drink, but Martin & Horton's gave him meals for the free publicity.

His afternoons would be spent in the libraries of the Bohemian Club, Mercantile Institute and Mechanic's Institute, reading books, playing chess exceptionally well, and writing proclamations on the Institute's handsomely engraved stationery. San Franciscans learned to ride the new "two-wheeled buggy" at a velocipedestrian school at the Mechanic's Pavilion. Someone took a picture of Norton riding a velocipede. He did not think the image befitted his imperial rank, and decreed that the sale of the picture be prohibited.

In the evenings, Norton went to debating societies, lectures and theater. One wag said that in San Francisco, you could see "Henry V" on stage and Norton I in the balcony.

Norton believed he had certain responsibilities as Emperor, so he visited schools and went to church every Sunday - Old St. Mary's one week and the First Unitarian Church another. On Saturday, he went to Temple Emanu-El. He told the Reverend O. P. Fitzgerald: "I think it is my duty to encourage religion and morality by showing myself at church and to avoid jealousy I attend them all in turn."

California was so split over the Civil War even preachers espoused one side or the other from the pulpit in their Sunday sermons. He said "I disapprove political preaching ... The preachers must stop preaching politics, or they must all come into one State Church. I will at once issue a decree to that effect."

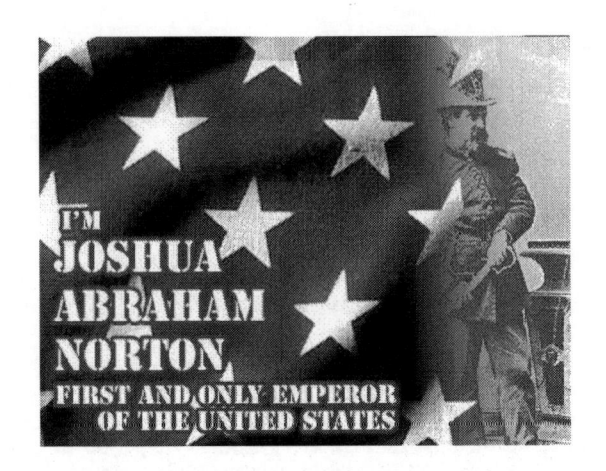

United States' First Emperor

He rode free on all the city's ferries and streetcars. Leland Stanford, President of the Central Pacific Railroad, gave Norton a free pass in California to offset his reputation as a greedy "robber baron." Norton used that free pass to attend sessions of the state legislature, sitting in the first row of the visitor's gallery, occasionally rattling his cane in commentary; and to review military troops around the Bay Area. When he tried to board the riverboat *Yosemite* for Sacramento in 1866, he was outraged that he was not allowed passage without a ticket. He sent a proclamation to the *Alta* ordering a *blockade of the Sacramento River* until the situation was set right.

Source of the Madness

There was one subtle irony that no one seemed to notice. Most royalty use the first name - Queen Mary, King Charles, Queen Victoria. But he was Norton the First. Indeed, after Norton first declared himself Emperor, he never used Joshua again.

In the late 1860s, Nathan Peiser had just arrived in San Francisco and was looking for a room. Peiser walked into the Eureka Lodgings, Norton's home of several years. In the hallway, Peiser saw Norton in his uniform. It would prove to be an incredible coincidence. Peiser *knew* Norton; he had met him 25 years earlier when Norton was still a clerk in his father's chandlery in Cape Town, South Africa. Peiser had spent almost a year with the Nortons recovering from injuries sustained when his ship was destroyed in a storm. Norton also recognized Peiser. In Norton's room they had the normal conversation of two people who had not seen each other in a quarter century. Peiser told the *Vallejo Chronicle* of their conversation.

Peiser recalled that 25 years earlier, Norton showed no interest in his father's religion; in fact, there was an incident where Norton disrupted his father's prayers meeting. Norton's first words to Peiser in 25 years were: "Why yes, Nathan, I distinctly remember you and the correction I received for raising a disturbance at a Jewish prayer meeting."

Then, Peiser asked Norton why he called himself Emperor and wore a uniform. Norton's demeanor suddenly changed. He went to the door, looked in the hallway, then locked the door. Whispering, he imposed a vow of silence on Peiser and revealed that he was not the son of John and Sarah Norton. He was of royal blood, a member of the Bourbon family of Kings who ruled France from 1589 until the French Revolution ended the reign of Louis the Sixteenth in 1793.

Many children of French royalty fled to England in the Revolution for safety, protected in the homes of commoners. When the Monarchy was restored under Louis the VIII in 1814, the newspapers were full of wild stories of people claiming to be forgotten heirs of royalty. The French credited England with helping to restore the Bourbons. Honored, many Brits gave their children French names.

Norton's parents had named their first son Lewis (not Louis), their third son was Philip and their second daughter Louisa. Although none of the other six Norton children, including Joshua, had French names, the young Joshua was convinced he was a royal given to the Norton family and his Jewish name was a clever way to protect the boy from assassins.

Norton told Peiser that he kept the name Norton out of love for the man who adopted him, but that the title of Emperor was rightfully his. Indeed, Norton claimed that Queen Victoria had presented his uniform. Peiser told Norton that he thought he was crazy. Norton replied: "and so do a good many others."

The Emperor as a National Character

Norton's fame would spread throughout the U.S. in the 1870's. The completion of the Transcontinental Railroad in 1869 connected America from Atlantic to Pacific, reducing a six-month journey by wagon or ship to only seven days. Now San Francisco was a tourist destination. Many knew about the Emperor from travel books and newspapers. When journalists from newspapers throughout the United States arrived to see and write about the city, they were unimpressed with the zoo at Woodward Gardens, or the seals and sea lions by the Cliff House. They preferred to write about Emperor Norton.

In 1876, Dom Pedro II, the Emperor of Brazil, visited San Francisco and asked to meet the Emperor of the United States. They met at a royal suite at the newly opened Palace Hotel and talked for more than an hour. In 1876, Dom Pedro II, the Emperor of Brazil, visited San Francisco and asked to meet the Emperor of the United States. They met at a royal suite at the newly opened Palace Hotel and talked for more than an hour. Dom Pedro never let on whether he realized that the United States really didn't have an emperor.

Benjamin Lloyd, in his book *Lights and Shades in San Francisco* let the tourists know that "He will talk very readily upon any subject, and his opinions are usually very correct, except when relating to himself. He is more familiar with history than the ordinary citizen, and his scientific knowledge, although sometimes mixed, is considerable."

Several cities tried to lure him away by sending him a gift of his favorite implement - a walking stick. Portland, Oregon sent an especially elaborate one called the Serpent Scepter, with a mahogany handle carved in the shape of a human hand grasping a snake.

But the press was also ridiculing his threadbare clothes. The Evening Express in Los Angeles called His Majesty "a walking travesty upon San Francisco's shoddy spirit." The local press, stung by the criticism, raised an outcry and the Board of Supervisors voted to buy the Emperor a new white beaver hat and officers coat.

Norton began issuing promissory notes that he called "Imperial Treasury Bond Certificates" in denominations of 50 cents to 10 dollars. He sold them to tourists and locals alike. Norton inscribed the notes with a promise they would be due and payable with 7% interest in the year of 1880. Of course, no one believed that. The real value was in the signature - a great souvenir of a visit to San Francisco.

And now just about every store in San Francisco had a sign saying "By Appointment to Norton I," and merchants made a killing selling picture postcards of the Emperor, Emperor Norton dolls complete with plumed hat, Emperor Norton cigars with his portrait on the label, and colored lithographs suitable for framing. One of the most popular items was a decade old lithograph of Norton standing at a buffet table, with two dogs looking longingly at him for a few scraps. It would become the source of the greatest myth of Emperor Norton.

By law, San Francisco destroyed stray dogs. But the Board of Supervisors adopted two as beloved city mascots: Bummer and Lazarus. They had but one notable quality - happily killing rats in a city teeming with them. They were rewarded with tasty morsels at the local taverns. Like Norton, they most enjoyed Martin & Horton's.

Edward Jump was a promising artist who earned a living drawing pictures for newspapers and magazines. Jump sold his drawing, called "The Three Bummers," to local merchants, who placed them as posters in their windows. Norton saw it in the window of a stationery store, and became enraged. One report has it that he broke the window with his cane and destroyed the drawing; another report has the window broke his walking stick.

When visitors asked merchants the story behind the drawing, it made far more sense to create that myth that Bummer and Lazarus were Norton's dogs, a myth that most San Franciscan's still believe today.

Madness or Genius?

But his madness did not always hide his genius. Because the Transcontinental Railroad's western terminus was Oakland, many feared that Oakland would eclipse San Francisco as the major city of the west. The Emperor had a solution. He issued this proclamation in 1872:

"The following is decreed and ordered to be carried into execution as soon as convenient: I. That a suspension bridge be built from Oakland Point to Goat Island and thence to Telegraph Hill; provided such bridge can be built without injury to navigable waters of the Bay of San Francisco. II. That the Central Pacific Railroad Company be granted franchises to lay down tracks and run cars from Telegraph Hill and along the city front to Mission Bay".

How prescient was Emperor Norton? 64 years later, the San Francisco Oakland Bay Bridge opened, a suspension bridge that passes through what we today call Yerba Buena Island, but in 1872 was Goat Island. The double decked freeway that once lined the Embarcadero from the foot of Broadway (at the base of Telegraph Hill) south to Mission Bay was officially part of the bridge!

The Central Pacific may have terminated in Oakland, but the destination markings on the trains said FRISCO. Norton didn't think that was very dignified for a city named for St. Francis. In 1872 issued the following edict:

"Whoever after due and proper warning shall be heard to utter the abominable word "Frisco", which has no linguistic or other warrant, shall be deemed guilty of a High Misdemeanor, and shall pay into the Imperial Treasury as penalty the sum of twenty-five dollars."

And now it was time to think about what had been missing all these years - an Empress. He was about 56 years old in 1874 when he became infatuated with a 16 year old high school girl graduate named Minnie Wakeman, who was described as "a tall, beautiful creature who had lovely dark blue eyes with fringed lashes and long curls that were the admiration of the whole school."

Norton wrote her a note that said: "My dear Miss Wakeman. In arranging for my Empress, I shall be delighted if you will permit me to make use of your name. Should you be willing, please let me know, but keep your own secret. It is safer that way, I think." He signed it - "Your devoted loving friend, The Emperor."

Unfortunately, Norton received a note thanking his majesty for graciously thinking her worthy of his attentions, but informing him that she was already engaged, which was true. There would be no Empress for the Emperor.

Le Roi Est Mort

The evening of January 8, 1880, was cold and rainy, as January days are so often in San Francisco. The Emperor was walking up California Street towards Nob Hill to attend the regular monthly debate of the Hastings Society at the Academy of Natural Sciences. As he neared Old St. Mary's Church, Norton staggered a bit, then slumped to the sidewalk. The reign of Norton I, Emperor of the United States and Protector of Mexico, expired with his final breath.

As a crowd gathered, the police moved his body to the city morgue. His clothes were as disheveled as always, and he had only a few coins on him - a gold piece worth $2.50, $3 in silver, and a French franc dated 1828, bearing the face of Charles X, France's last Bourbon king. He had a bundle of his 50 cent imperial treasury notes, dated for repayment in 1890. He intended to exchange these notes for his original notes, due and payable this very month, which he could not have honored.

He also had telegrams from the Czar Alexander II of Russia that said "we approve heartily and congratulate you" on his impending marriage to Queen Victoria. Another from the President of the French Republic said, "we understand that Queen Victoria will propose marriage to you as a means of uniting England the United States. Consider well, and do not accept. No good will come of it." These were, of course, hoaxes, an example of some people having fun at the expense of the Emperor.

The next morning, the headline in the *Chronicle* screamed: "Le Roi Est Mort" (The King is dead). *The Alta California* printed a 34-inch story on the same day it devoted all of 38 words - a mere 4-lines of type - from the inaugural speech of George C. Perkins, newly elected Governor of California.

The leading papers of Cleveland, Seattle, Denver, Philadelphia, and Portland, reported his death. The Cincinnati Enquirer devoted 16 inches, under a headline that said, in part, "An emperor without enemies, a king without a kingdom, supported in life by the willing tribute of a free people."

At his home in Hartford, Connecticut, Mark Twain read of the Emperor's death in the New York Times. He sadly wrote to a good friend, fellow acclaimed novelist, and Editor of the *Atlantic Monthly*, William Dean Howells: "What an odd thing it is that neither Frank Soulé, nor Charley Warren Stoddard, nor I, nor Bret Harte, the Immortal Bilk, nor any other professionally literary person in San Francisco has ever 'written up' the Emperor Norton.

10,000 people came to see Emperor Norton lying in state at the morgue. Jimmy Bowman, of the San Francisco Chronicle wrote. "The visitors included all classes from the capitalist to the pauper, the clergyman and the pickpocket, well dressed ladies, the bowed with age, and the prattling child."

James Eastland, President of the Pacific Club, was one of the leading businessmen who knew Norton in the early, prosperous years. They were both members of the Freemasons. Eastland could not envision Norton buried in a pauper's grave. He raised all the money deemed necessary from his club for a funeral fit for an Emperor and burial at the Masonic Cemetery.

A funeral cortege followed Norton's body from the morgue to the cemetery that was two miles long. As they lay his body into the ground, the world grew dark with that phenomenon of infrequent occurrence, a total eclipse of the sun.

In 1934, San Francisco closed all its cemeteries to make more space for the living. Norton was re-interred with civic and military honors at Woodlawn Memorial Park in Colma.

Throughout San Francisco there are small tributes to Emperor Norton. A group called E Clampus Vitus, established to help widows and orphans of gold and silver miners, created a plaque to honor him that was originally in the Cliff House, but now is on the entrance on the Transbay Terminal on Mission Street. They also celebrate his birthday every year with a great party by his grave. The Harbor Emperor is a ferry with a carved Emperor Norton masthead, there is an Emperor Norton Inn, and a few other sites bear his name.

Emperor Norton is remembered in literature. In *The Adventures of Huckleberry Finn*, Mark Twain created the character of "the king" based on Norton. Robert Louis Stevenson included Norton as an actual character in his 1892 novel, *The Wrecker*.

The stepdaughter of Robert Louis Stevenson, Isobel Field, wrote about Norton in her book entitled *This Life I've Loved*: "He was a gentle and kindly man, and fortunately found himself in the friendliest and most sentimental city in the world, the idea being 'let him be emperor if he wants to.' San Francisco played the game with him."

Alcatraz

Alcatraz Island is located in the San Francisco Bay, 1.5 miles offshore from San Francisco. Often referred to as "The Rock", the small island was developed with facilities for a lighthouse, a military fortification, a military prison (1868), and a federal prison from 1933 until 1963. Beginning in November 1969, the island was occupied for more than 19 months by a group of American Indians from San Francisco who were part of a wave of Indian activism across the nation with public protests through the 1970s. In 1972 Alcatraz became a national recreation area and received designation as a National Historic Landmark in 1986.

Alcatraz

During its 29 years of operation, the penitentiary claimed no prisoner had successfully escaped. A total of 36 prisoners made 14 escape attempts, two men trying twice; 23 were caught, six were shot and killed during their escape, two drowned, and five are listed as "missing and presumed drowned". The most violent occurred on May 2, 1946, when a failed escape attempt by six prisoners led to the Battle of Alcatraz.

Angel Island

Sometimes called the Ellis Island of the West, the Angel Island immigration station was not precisely a West Coast counterpart of the East Coast's main immigrant processing center. In fact, owing to the anti-Asian immigration laws in force during the center's years of operation, Angel Island officials often devoted themselves to keeping newcomers out of the United States, rather than welcoming them in.

Angel Island Immigration Station

After 1910, immigration officials at Angel Island developed elaborate procedures to identify and deport would-be immigrants from China who sought ways around the ban on their immigration. The immigrants knew that the Exclusion Act could not apply to the children of American citizens, so if Chinese Americans born in the United States had offspring in China, those children should have the legal right to enter the United States. After many public records were destroyed by San Francisco's great earthquake and fire of 1906, it became common for young men in China to buy documents that identified them as American citizens by claiming U.S.-born Chinese men as their fathers. Immigration officials at Angel Island had no way to tell "paper sons" from real sons, so they detained many male immigrants for weeks or months and tried to expose them as frauds by quizzing them in minute detail about such topics as family histories and ancestral villages. Typical interrogations included questions about habits or facial characteristics of relatives and odd bits of information about the histories and customs of the home villages. Immigrants prepared for weeks for the dreaded Angel Island interrogations, which were conducted through interpreters and could result in deportation because of misunderstandings or miscommunication. Chinese women immigrating as wives or daughters of American-born Chinese experienced similar detentions and interrogation. Whole families in detention were frequently separated and housed according to sex, a policy that was particularly hard on young children.

Fort Point

Fort Point is located at the southern side of the Golden Gate at the entrance to San Francisco Bay. This fort was completed just before the American Civil War, to defend San Francisco Bay against hostile warships.

The U.S. Army Corps of Engineers began work on Fort Point in 1853. Plans specified that the lowest tier of artillery be as close as possible to water level so cannonballs could ricochet across the water's surface to hit enemy ships at the waterline. Workers blasted the 90-foot cliff down to 15 feet above sea level. The structure featured seven-foot-thick walls and multi-tiered casemated construction typical of Third System forts. It was sited to defend the maximum amount of harbor area. While there were more than 30 such forts on the East Coast, Fort Point was the only one on the West Coast. In 1854 Inspector General Joseph K. Mansfield declared "this point as the key to the whole Pacific Coast...and it should receive untiring exertions".

A crew of 200, many unemployed miners, labored for eight years on the fort. In 1861, with war looming, the Army mounted the fort's first cannon. Col. Albert Sidney Johnston, commander of the Department of the Pacific, prepared Bay Area defenses and ordered in the first troops to the fort. Kentucky-born Johnston then resigned his commission to join the Confederate Army; he was killed at the Battle of Shiloh in 1862.

Throughout the Civil War, artillerymen at Fort Point stood guard for an enemy that never came. The Confederate raider CSS Shenandoah planned to attack San Francisco, but on the way to the harbor the captain learned that the war was over; it was August 1865, months after General Lee surrendered.

Fort Point

Golden Gate Bridge

The Golden Gate Bridge is a suspension bridge spanning the Golden Gate, the opening of the San Francisco Bay into the Pacific Ocean. As part of both U.S. Route 101 and California State Route 1, the structure links the city of San Francisco, on the northern tip of the San Francisco Peninsula, to Marin County. It is one of the most internationally recognized symbols of San Francisco, California, and the United States. It has been declared one of the modern Wonders of the World by the American Society of Civil Engineers. The Frommers travel guide considers the Golden Gate Bridge "possibly the most beautiful, certainly the most photographed, bridge in the world".

Golden Gate Bridge

    Construction began on January 5, 1933. When completed in 1937, the Golden Gate Bridge had the longest suspension bridge main span in the world, at 4,200 feet. Since 1964, its main span length has been surpassed by eight other bridges. However, it still has the second longest main span in the United States, after the Verrazano-Narrows Bridge in New York City. The total length of the Golden Gate Bridge, including approaches from abutment to abutment, is 8,981 feet. At 692 feet above water, the Golden Gate Bridge also had the world's tallest suspension towers when built. It held that status until 1998, with the completion of bridges in Denmark and Japan.

    The weight of the roadway is hung from two cables that pass through the two main towers and are fixed in concrete at each end. Each cable is made of 27,572 strands of wire. There are 80,000 miles of wire in the main cables. The bridge has approximately 1,200,000 total rivets.

Golden Gate Bridge

The bridge was originally painted with red lead primer and a lead-based topcoat, which was touched up as required. In the mid-1960s, a program was started to improve corrosion protection by stripping the original paint and repainting the bridge with zinc silicate primer and vinyl topcoats. Since 1990 acrylic topcoats have been used instead for air-quality reasons. The program was completed in 1995 and it is now maintained by 38 painters who touch up the paintwork where it becomes seriously coroded.

Muir Woods National Monument

Muir Woods National Monument is a unit of the National Park Service on the Pacific coast of southwestern Marin County, 12 miles north of San Francisco and part of the Golden Gate National Recreation Area. It protects 554 acres of which 240 acres are old growth Coast Redwood (*Sequoia sempervirens*) forests, one of a few such stands remaining in the San Francisco Bay Area.

Muir Woods

The star attraction of the Muir Woods is the Coast Redwood. These relatives of the Giant Sequoia are known for their height. While redwoods can grow to nearly 380 feet tall, the tallest tree in the Muir Woods is 258 feet. The trees come from a seed no bigger than that of a tomato's. The average age of the redwoods in the Monument are between 500 and 800 years old with the oldest being at least 1,200 years old.

John Muir (21 April 1838 – 24 December 1914) was a Scottish-born American naturalist, author, and early advocate of preservation of wilderness in the United States. His letters, essays, and books telling of his adventures in nature, especially in the Sierra Nevada mountains of California have been read by millions. His activism helped to save the Yosemite Valley, Sequoia National Park and other wilderness areas. The Sierra Club, which he founded, is now one of the most important conservation organizations in the United States. One of the most well-known hiking trails in the U.S., the 211-mile John Muir Trail, was named in his honor.

Other places named in his honor are Muir Woods National Monument, Muir Beach, John Muir College, Mount Muir, Camp Muir and Muir Glacier.

John Muir

In his later life, Muir devoted most of his time to the preservation of the Western forests. He petitioned the U.S. Congress for the National Park bill that was passed in 1890, establishing both Yosemite and Sequoia National Parks. Because of the spiritual quality and enthusiasm toward nature expressed in his writings, he was able to inspire readers, including presidents and congressmen, to take action to help preserve large nature areas. He is today referred to as the "Father of the National Parks," and the National Park Service produced a short documentary on his life.

Muir's biographer, Steven J. Holmes, states that Muir has become "one of the patron saints of twentieth-century American environmental activity," both political and recreational. As a result, his writings are commonly discussed in books and journals, and he is often quoted in books by nature photographers such as Ansel Adams. "Muir has profoundly shaped the very categories through which Americans understand and envision their relationships with the natural world," writes Holmes. Muir was noted for being an ecological thinker, political spokesman, and religious prophet, whose writings became a personal guide into nature for countless individuals, making his name "almost ubiquitous" in the modern environmental consciousness. According to author William Anderson, Muir exemplified "the archetype of our oneness with the earth", while biographer Donald Worster says he believed his mission was "...saving the American soul from total surrender to materialism."

Fort Ross

Fort Ross (Russian: Форт-Росс), originally Fortress Ross' (Крепость Россъ, r *Krepost' Ross'*) is a former Russian establishment in what is now Sonoma County. It was the hub of the southernmost Russian settlements in North America between 1812 to 1842. It has been the subject of archaeological investigation and is a National Historic Landmark and on the National Register of Historic Places. It is part of California's Fort Ross State Historic Park.

Fort Ross is a landmark in the history of European imperialism. The Spanish expansion went west across the Atlantic Ocean and the Russian expansion went east across Siberia and the Pacific Ocean. In the early nineteenth century, the two waves of expansion met on the opposite side of the world along the Pacific Coast of California, with Russia arriving from the north and Spain from the south. The United States of America arrived in 1846 from the east.

State Route 1 once bisected Fort Ross. It entered from the northeast where the Kuskov House once stood, and exited through the main gate to the southwest. The road was eventually diverted, and the parts of the fort that had been demolished for the road were rebuilt. The old roadway can still be seen going from the main gate to the northwest; the rest (within the fort and extending northeast) has been removed.

Most of the existing buildings on the site are reconstructions. Cooperative research efforts with Russian archives will help to correct interpretive errors present in structures that date from the Cold-War period. The only original structure remaining is the Rotchev House. Known as the "Commandant's House" from the 1940s through the 1970s, it was the residence of the last manager, Aleksandr Rotchev. Renovated in 1836 from an existing structure, it was titled the "new commandant's house" in the

1841 inventory to differentiate it from the "old commandant's house" (Kuskov House). The Rotchev House, or in original documents, "Administrator's House", is at the center of efforts to "re-interpret" Russia's part in California's colonial history. The Fort Ross Interpretive Association has received several federally funded grants to restore both exterior and interior elements.

Fort Ross

Kruse Rhododendron State Reserve

This pristine reserve contains 317 acres of second-growth redwood, Douglas fir, grand firs, tanoaks, and a plethora of rhododendrons. Each May these spectacular flowers burst into bloom and color the deep green of the forest with brilliant pink blossoms.

The wealth of rhododendrons in this reserve is a direct result of normal plant succession patterns following a severe fire that once occurred here. Today, the regenerating forest is gradually overwhelming the rhododendrons. As forests constantly evolve, plants compete for available sunlight, water and nutrients and the best suited species dominate the environment until they create conditions more conducive to the success of other plant populations. In order to maintain fine displays of rhododendron blooms, the current plant succession must be slowed, which is the goal the Department of Parks and Recreation in its management of the reserve. To achieve this goal, the tanoak trees have been thinned out and the rhododendrons revived with the renewal pruning practices. This has ensured vigorous new growth and a diversity of blooming heights. When the rejuvenation project began during the fall of 1979, there were few blooms, and those that did appear were all well above eye level. Tanoaks were crowding out the rhododendrons by successfully competing for available sunlight, resulting in rangy growth habits of the rhododendrons. Final major pruning occurred in the fall of 1981. By 1984 a significant increase in the floral displays was evident.

Kruse Rhododendron State Reserve

Sea Ranch

Sea Ranch is located along the Pacific Coast, about 100 mi north of San Francisco and 120 mi west of Sacramento. Sea Ranch is reached by way of State Route 1.

Architect and planner Al Boeke envisioned a community that would preserve the area's natural beauty. Boeke first surveyed the land in 1962. In 1963, Oceanic California Inc., a division of Castle and Cooke Inc., and assembled a design team. Halprin created the master plan for Sea Ranch, which grew to encompass 10 miles of the Sonoma County coastline.

Sea Ranch

The project met opposition that led to notable changes in California law. While the County Board of Supervisors initially regarded the developer's offer to dedicate 140 acres for public parkland as sufficient, opponents felt more coastal access was necessary. The site, containing 10 miles of shore, had been available to the public but would be reserved for private use under the developer's plan. Areas below high tide were and would remain public property, but the plan provided no access through the development. In addition, California's coast at the time was only open to the public along 100 of its 1,300 miles.

Californians Organized to Acquire Access to State Tidelands (COAST) was formed in response to this issue, and their 1968 county ballot initiative attempted to require the development to include public trails to the tidelands. While the initiative did not pass, the California legislature's Dunlap Act did pass that year and required that new coastal development dedicate trails granting public access to the ocean. This episode led to the establishment of the Coastal Alliance, an organization of 100 groups similar to COAST, that placed Proposition 20 on the statewide 1972 ballot. The initiative passed, and it established the California Coastal Commission, which continues to regulate land use on the California coast.

Mendocino

Mendocino is an unincorporated community in Mendocino County. Mendocino is located 9.5 miles south of Fort Bragg, at an elevation of 154 feet. The town's name comes from Cape Mendocino, named by early Spanish navigators in honor of Antonio de Mendoza, Viceroy of New Spain. Despite its small size, the town's scenic location on a headland surrounded by the Pacific Ocean has made it extremely popular as an artist colony and with vacationers.

Most of the town was added to the National Register of Historic Places listings in Mendocino County, in 1971 as the Mendocino and Headlands Historic District. Mendocino Presbyterian Church on Main Street, dedicated on July 5, 1868, is one of the oldest continuously-used Protestant churches in California and is designated as a California historical landmark. In addition, the Temple of Kwan Tai on Albion Street, may be as old as 1854 and is one of the oldest Chinese houses of worship in California.

Temple of Kwan Tai

Skunk Train

The California Western Railroad (reporting mark CWR), popularly called the Skunk Train, is a heritage railroad in Mendocino County, running from the railroad's headquarters in the coastal town of Fort Bragg, and the interchange with the Northwestern Pacific Railroad at Willits.

The CWR runs steam and diesel-powered trains and rail motor cars 40 miles through Redwood forests along Pudding Creek and the Noyo River. Along the way, the tracks cross some 30 bridges and trestles and pass through two deep mountain tunnels. The halfway point of Northspur is a popular meals and beverage spot for the railroad's passengers when locomotives turn around before returning trains to their respective terminals.

Skunk Train

Gas-powered, self propelled, passenger railcars were added in 1925 and CWR steam passenger trains were mostly eliminated. These motorcars were nicknamed "Skunks" because people said "You can smell 'em before you can see 'em." In 1965 the line reintroduced summer steam passenger service between Fort Bragg and Willits with Baldwin-built steam locomotive No.45, calling the colorful train "The Super Skunk." That train was discontinued in 2001, then revived in September 2006 as a special event train. No.45 continues to power excursion trains from Fort Bragg, as far as Northspur the CWR's mid-point, on selected weekends summer to early autumn.

Avenue of the Giants

The Avenue of the Giants is a scenic highway running through Humboldt Redwoods State Park. It is an old alignment of U.S. Route 101, and continues to be maintained by the state as State Route 254.

The southern entrance to the Avenue is just north of Garberville, and the northern entrance is south of Fortuna. The highway is notable for the Coast Redwoods that overshadow the road and surround the area. It is from these towering trees that the Avenue of the Giants takes its name. The road winds alongside the scenic Eel River, and connects several small towns such as Phillipsville, Miranda, Myers Flat, Burlington, Weott, Englewood, Redcrest and Pepperwood.

Avenue of the Giants

Founder's Grove, near Weott, this grove has an easy 1/2 mile self-guided walk with informational booklets available at the beginning of the trail. This well-travelled trail is a good example of old-growth redwood forest and contains a few very big trees, including the Founder's Tree, 346 ft. tall.

Avenue of the Giants features three trees in Northern California that visitors can drive through. The southernmost of these trees, Chandelier Tree, is located in Drive-Thru Tree Park in the town of Leggett. Shrine Drive-Thru Tree is near the town of Myers Flat and Klamath Tour Thru Tree, the northernmost of the three trees, is located in the town of Klamath. Each tree is privately owned and charges $5 or more to drive through.

Scotia

Scotia is a company town which was previously wholly owned by the Pacific Lumber Company (PALCO). While it is home to approximately 800 past or present mill employees and their dependents, a process is underway to divide the homes into lots for sale. Located in Humboldt County, its partially wooded hillside near the Eel River is highlighted by the sheer size of mammoth lumber mill buildings located between the town and the river. Via U.S. Route 101, the town is 28 miles south of Eureka, and 244 miles north of San Francisco.

Scotia was founded in 1863 as Forestville and renamed 25 years later. At the time of its founding, Scotia was just one of many company towns across the Pacific Northwest, many of which closed down during the Great Depression. Scotia, however, was one of a relative handful of company towns to survive this period. Most of the existing homes were built between the 1920s and 1950s.

Scotia

Carson Mansion

The Carson Mansion is a large Victorian house located in Old Town, Eureka. Regarded as one of the highest executions of American Queen Anne Style architecture, the home is "considered the most grand Victorian home in America It is one of the most written about and photographed Victorian houses in California and perhaps, in the United States. Originally the home of one of Northern California's first major lumber barons, it has housed the Ingomar Club, a private members only club, since 1950. Though the front and south-side elevations can be easily viewed from the public street and sidewalk, the home and grounds are never open to the general public.

The mansion is a mix of every major style of Victorian Architecture, including but not limited to the following styles: Eastlake, Italianate, Queen Anne (primary), and Stick, depending on which expert one consults. One nationally known architectural historian described the home as "a baronial castle in Redwood..." and stated further that "The illusion of grandeur in the house is heightened by the play on scale, the use of fanciful detail and the handling of mass as separate volumes, topped by a lively roofscape." A nationally recognized architectural survey stated, "The home epitomizes the range of possibilities for eclectic design expression" in the use of Victorian architectural styles in a manner that is "peculiarily American." Unlike most other homes dating from the period, this property has always been meticulously maintained, therefore standing today in virtually the same condition as when it was built.

The Carson Mansion is included in the Historic American Buildings Survey (HABS) as Catalog number CA-1911. Completed in May 1964, this is the only official historical building listing in the State of California and nationally architecturally significant structure. Though it merits National Register of Historic Places status, the Ingomar Club does not open the home and grounds to the public, nor has it applied for National Register Status.

Carson Mansion

Section 6

Eureka to South Lake Tahoe

California 255 to US 101 to California 299 to California 96 to Interstate 5 to US 97 to California 161 to California 139 to California 299 to US 395 to California 70 to California 49 to California 89 to California 267 to California 28 to California 89

Samoa

Samoa is located in the northern peninsula of Humboldt Bay. The name Samoa is used interchangeably with the peninsula it occupies. It is the site of the Samoa Cookhouse, the last remaining original, lumber style cookhouses, where once you walk through the door, you will take a step back into the early days of the lumber and logging industry. As the last surviving cookhouse of the west, all meals are still served "lumber camp" style. The food is brought to the table in large bowls and platters. Inside is also a complimentary museum full of relics and photographs from the old logging and Cookhouse days. The walls are lined with an extensive pictorial review of this history, including the maritime industry.

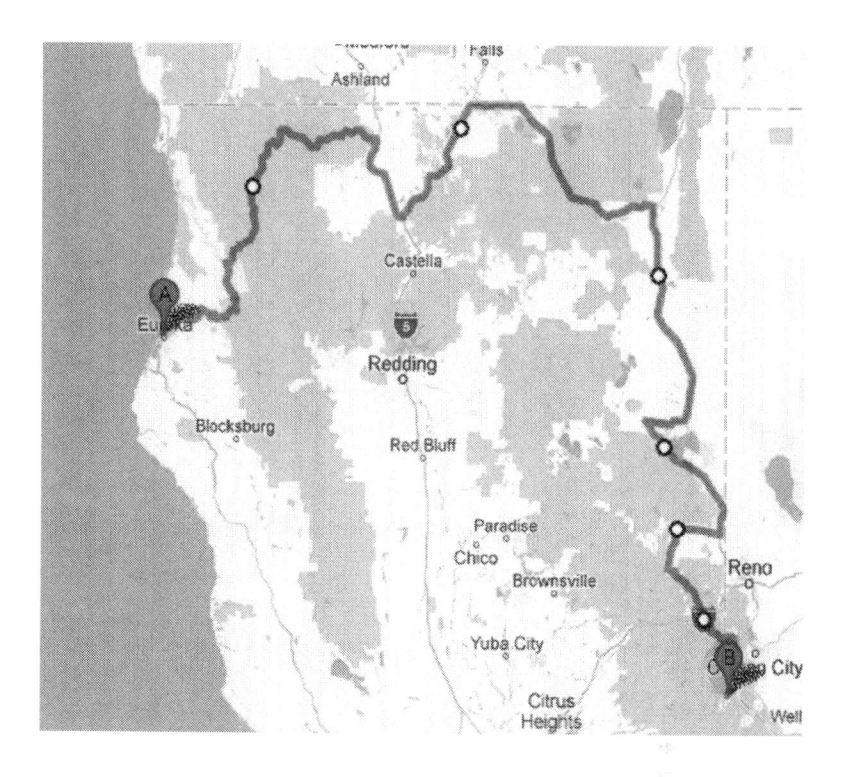

Eureka to South Lake Tahoe (Google Maps)

Samoa Cookhouse

Pythian Castle

The Pythian Castle building in Arcata, is a Queen Anne architecture styled building built in 1885. It was listed on the National Register of Historic Places in 1986. A Pythian Castle was a local meeting place of the Knights of Pythias, a fraternal organization and secret society founded at Washington, DC, on 19 February 1864. A member must be at least 18 years of age. He cannot be a professional gambler, or involved with illegal drugs or alcohol and he must have a belief in a Supreme Being.

Pythian Castle

Mad River

The Mad River flows for 113 miles in a roughly northwest direction through Trinity County and then Humboldt County, draining a 497-square-mile watershed into the Pacific Ocean. The river's headwaters are in the Coast Range near South Kelsey Ridge. The river was named in December, 1849 in memory of an incident when Dr. Josiah Gregg lost his temper when his gold exploration party did not wait for him at the river mouth.

The Mad River, is rated as a class III-V whitewater river. The natural beauty of California and the beautiful way the water current moves down the stream is marvelous. Whitewater rafting and kayaking spots in California are harder than the national norm, so keep in mind that many of the rivers here are not very forgiving. The starting location is a reasonable drive from Eureka-Arcata-Fortuna. The beauty of the Coast Ranges is a great plus for this river. If you hurry you can run the top section in a day. There are a number of good spots for whitewater rafting, kayaking, and other stretches that can be paddled.

Mad River

Bigfoot

Bigfoot, also known as sasquatch, is an ape-like cryptid that purportedly inhabits forests, mainly in the Pacific Northwest region of North America. Bigfoot is usually described as a large, hairy, bipedal humanoid. The term "sasquatch" is an anglicized derivative of the Halkomelem word *sásq'ets*.

Bigfoot

Bigfoot is described in reports as a large hairy ape-like creature, in a range of 6–10 feet tall, weighing in excess of 500 pounds, and covered in dark brown or dark reddish hair. Alleged witnesses have described large eyes, a pronounced brow ridge, and a large, low-set forehead; the top of the head has been described as rounded and crested, similar to the sagittal crest of the male gorilla. Bigfoot is commonly reported to have a strong, unpleasant smell by those who claim to have encountered it. The enormous footprints for which it is named have been as large as 24 inches long and 8 inches wide. While most casts have five toes — like all known apes — some casts of alleged bigfoot tracks have had numbers ranging from two to six. Some have also contained claw marks, making it likely that a portion came from known animals such as bears, which have five toes and claws. Some proponents have also claimed that bigfoot is omnivorous and mainly nocturnal.

Bigfoot proponents Grover Krantz and Geoffrey Bourne believe that Bigfoot could be a relict population of *Gigantopithecus*. Bourne contends that as most *Gigantopithecus* fossils are found in China, and as many species of animals migrated across the Bering land bridge, it is not unreasonable to assume that *Gigantopithecus* might have as well.

Willow Creek, is known as the Gateway to Bigfoot Country, and the beginning of California 96, the Bigfoot Scenic Byway.

Trinity Alps

The Trinity Alps are mountains in Northern California, in the Pacific Coast Ranges physiographic region. Elevations there range from 1,350 feet to 8,994 ft at Thompson Peak. The Trinity Alps Wilderness covers 517,000 acres, making it the second largest wilderness area in California. The area was formerly known as the Salmon-Trinity Alps Primitive Area since 1932 until a series of expansions. The Trinity Alps are situated within the Klamath Mountains Range, which lies between the Pacific Coast Ranges to the west and the Cascade Range further to the east. The Trinity Alps are noted for their scenic views and alpine environment, which differ from those found in the Sierra Nevada, the Coastal Range, or the Cascades. The northern backbone of these mountains is the Salmon and Scott Mountains.

On the ridge south of Sapphire Lake is an unusual phenomenon consisting of a temporary glacier, versus an inactive snowfield that melts out in dry years. Following years of heavy accumulation, an icefield appears in this fully sheltered north-facing cirque that can show active crevasses and seracs some tens of feet high. But this ice body, at an elevation of only 7,500 feet in a region experiencing a long, hot dry season from about mid May to mid October, can disappear completely during a run of drier years. The lowest snowfield in California that does not disappear except in the extreme runs of dry years is located above Mirror Lake at an elevation of 6,600 feet. Studies of lichen collars indicate that the site near Kalmia Lake is the snowiest spot in the State of California, receiving snow accumulation in excess of the Lake Helen snowcourse on Lassen Peak, by far the snowcourse with greatest late winter snow accumulation in California. This in turn is consistent with the fact of an active glacier under Thompson Peak, while, in contrast, no such active glacier exists under Brokeoff Mountain west of Lassen Peak, higher than Thompson Peak and presenting an ideal NNE-facing zone in the area of maximum snow accumulation beneath an almost-vertical cliff face 1,000 feet high. Sufficient snow does accumulate under Brokeoff that in some years the snowfield there experiences

Trinity Alps

incipient glacial motion. Two moraines below it, one very recent, provide clear evidence at least of mass transport in the recent past at that site. These moraines are quite a bit smaller than those found below the Thompson Peak glacieret.

Yreka Bakery

Mark Twain, in his *Autobiography* (p. 162, Harper/Perennial Literary, 1990), tells how Yreka got its name. There was a bakeshop with a canvas sign which had not yet been put up but had been painted and stretched to dry in such a way that the word BAKERY, all but the B, showed through and was reversed. A stranger read it wrong end first, YREKA, and supposed that that was the name of the camp. The campers were satisfied with it and adopted it.

Original Yreka Bakery

Mt. Shasta

Mount Shasta (*Úytaahkoo* in Karuk or "White Mountain") is located at the southern end of the Cascade Range in Siskiyou County. At 14,179 feet is the second highest peak in the Cascades and the fifth highest in California. Mount Shasta has an estimated volume of 85 cubic miles which makes it the most voluminous stratovolcano in the Cascade Volcanic Arc.

Mt. Shasta

About 593,000 years ago, andesitic lavas erupted in what is now Mount Shasta's western flank near McBride Spring. Over time, an ancestral Mount Shasta stratovolcano was built to a large but unknown height; sometime between 300,000 and 360,000 years ago the entire north side of the volcano collapsed, creating an enormous landslide or debris avalanche, 6.5 cu mi in volume. The slide flowed northwestward into Shasta Valley, where the Shasta River now cuts through the 28-mile-long flow.

Mount Shasta's surface is relatively free of deep glacial erosion except, paradoxically, for its south side where Sargents Ridge runs parallel to the U-shaped Avalanche Gulch. This is the largest glacial valley on the volcano, although it does not presently have a glacier in it. There are seven named glaciers on Mount Shasta, with the four largest (Whitney, Bolam, Hotlum, and Wintun) radiating down from high on the main summit cone to below 10,000 ft primarily on the north and east sides. The Whitney Glacier is the longest and the Hotlum is the most voluminous glacier in the state of California. Three of the smaller named glaciers occupy cirques near and above 11,000 ft on the south and southeast sides, including the Watkins, Konwakiton, and Mud Creek Glaciers.

Whitney Glacier

What remains of the oldest of Mount Shasta's four cones is exposed at Sargents Ridge on the south side of the mountain. Lavas from the Sargents Ridge vent cover the Everitt Hill shield at Mount Shasta's southern foot. The last lavas to erupt from the vent were hornblende-pyroxene andesites with a hornblende dacite dome at its summit. Glacial erosion has since modified its shape.

The next cone to form is exposed south of Mount Shasta's current summit and is called Misery Hill. It was formed 15,000 to 20,000 years ago from pyroxene andesite flows and has since been intruded by a hornblende dacite dome.

Since then the Shastina cone has been built by mostly pyroxene andesite lava flows. Some 9,500 years ago, these flows reached about 6.8 mi south and 3 mi north of the area now occupied by nearby Black Butte. The last eruptions formed Shastina's present summit about a hundred years later. But before that, Shastina, along with the then forming Black Butte dacite plug dome complex to the west, created numerous pyroclastic flows that covered 43 sq mi, including large parts of what are now the towns of Mount Shasta, and Weed. Diller Canyon 400 ft deep and 0.25 mi wide is an avalanche chute that was probably carved into Shastina's western face by these flows.

The last to form, and the highest cone, the Hotlum Cone, formed about 8,000 years ago. It is named after the Hotlum glacier on its northern face; its longest lava flow, the 500 ft-thick Military Pass flow, extends 5.5 mi down its northwest face. Since the creation of the Hotlum Cone, a dacite dome intruded the cone and now forms the summit. The rock at the 600 ft-wide summit crater has been extensively hydrothermally altered by sulfurous hot springs and fumaroles there (only a few examples still remain).

In the last 8,000 years, the Hotlum Cone has erupted at least eight or nine times. About 200 years ago the last significant Mount Shasta eruption came from this cone and created a pyroclastic flow, a hot lahar (mudflow), and three cold lahars, which streamed 7.5 mi down Mount Shasta's east flank via Ash Creek. A separate hot lahar went 12 mi down Mud Creek. This eruption was observed by the explorer La Pérouse, from his ship off the California coast, in 1786.

Tule Lake Internment Center

Tule Lake Internment Center was an internment camp in the town of Newell near Tule Lake. It was used in the Japanese American internment during World War II. It was the largest (in terms of population) and most controversial of the camps, and did not close until after the war, in 1946. In December 2008 it was designated by President George W. Bush as one of nine sites—the only one in the contiguous 48 states—to be part of the new World War II Valor in the Pacific National Monument.

Among the Japanese Americans interned at Tule Lake were internees from other camps who refused to take a vow of undivided loyalty to the U.S. and were sent to this "Segregation Camp," or had given answers on the loyalty questionnaire that suggested they were untrustworthy or security risks. As a result, it had the highest level of security of any of the camps. Many loyal Americans of Japanese ancestry were first interned there before this camp became known as the "NO NO" Camp. These loyal Americans of Japanese ancestry were later sent off to more permanent "Concentration Camps" such as Heart Mountain, WY. and Topaz, UT.

At the beginning of the internment, Japanese Americans and resident aliens of Japanese descent were given a questionnaire to determine their loyalty to the United States. Question 27 on the questionnaire asked, "Are you willing to serve in the armed forces of the United States on combat duty, wherever ordered?" while question 28 asked, "Will you swear unqualified allegiance to the United States and faithfully defend the United States from any or all attack by foreign or domestic forces, and forswear any form of allegiance or obedience to the Japanese emperor, or any other foreign government, power, or organization?"

Tule Lake Internment Center

A number of those who were sent to Tule Lake had found the loyalty oath's questions confusing, while others, certain that they were to be deported to Japan no matter how they had answered, feared that answering the questions in the affirmative would cause them to be seen as enemy aliens by the Japanese. Others chose to answer "no" to both questions in protest of their imprisonment.

Some of the Tule Lake internees had participated in demonstrations against the internment policy at other camps. Many residents had renounced their U.S. citizenship, often due to deception or coercion. Most of the Tule Lake renunciants later had their citizenship restored, largely through the vigorous efforts of civil rights attorney Wayne M. Collins.

Unsanitary, squalid living conditions, inadequate medical care, poor food, and unsafe working conditions had prompted protests at several camps. In November 1943 a series of meetings and protests over poor living conditions at Tule Lake prompted the Army to impose martial law over the camp.

Tule Lake Internment Center

Starting in 1974, Tule Lake was the site of several pilgrimages by activists calling for an official apology from the U.S. government. This Redress Movement culminated in the Civil Liberties Act of 1988. The pilgrimages, serving educational purposes, continue to this day.

On December 21, 2006 U.S. President George W. Bush signed H.R. 1492 into law guaranteeing $38,000,000 in federal money to restore the Tule Lake relocation center along with nine other former Japanese internment camps. In December 2008 it was designated by President George W. Bush as one of nine sites—the only one in the contiguous 48 states—to be part of the new World War II Valor in the Pacific National Monument.

Lava Beds National Monument

Lava Beds National Monument is located in Siskiyou and Modoc Counties. The Monument lies on the northeastern flank of the Medicine Lake Volcano, with the largest total area covered by a volcano in the Cascade Range. The region in and around Lava Beds Monument is unique because it lies on the junction of the Sierra-Klamath, Cascade, and the Great Basin physiographic provinces. The Monument was established as a United States National Monument on November 21, 1925, including over 46,000 acres.

Lava Beds National Monument has numerous lava tube caves, with twenty five having marked entrances and developed trails for public access and exploration. The monument also offers trails through the high Great Basin xeric shrubland desert landscape and the volcanic fields.

Lava Tube

Lava flows dated to about 30,000-40,000 years ago formed most of the lava tube caves in the monument. As the hot basaltic lava flowed downhill, the top cooled and crusted over, insulating the rest of the lava and forming lava tubes. Lavacicles on the ceiling of a lava tube were left as the level of lava in the tube retreated and the viscous lava on the ceiling dripped as it cooled.

Dripstone was created when lava splashed on the inside walls of the tubes. The leaching of minerals from pumice gravel, soils, and overlying rock provides for deposition of secondary speleothems in lava tubes.

Lava Beds National Monument has the largest concentration of lava tube caves in North America. One has electrical lighting, the others are illuminated by ceiling collapse portals or require flashlights, available to loan.

Termo

Termo is an unincorporated community in Lassen County. It is located on the Southern Pacific Railroad 32 miles north-northeast of Susanville, at an elevation of 5305 feet This town straddles U.S. Highway 395 north of Ravendale. In 1909, Termo was the terminus of the Nevada–California –Oregon Railway. The Termo post office opened in 1908, closed in 1914, and re-opened in 1915.

Termo

This is a town that time forgot and the village that is Termo will be the place you will recall for quite some time after you depart. There is not much in the area but for a quick visit it is ideal especially because of the rich history it has so much of. It would seem like this could not hold a load of history being that it is in the middle of nowhere but that would not be the reality. The truth is that a stay even a camping out adventure in the town would be a really fun and exciting endeavor for the entire family. The town of Termo although incredibly small and very isolated is still a fine location for a family camping trip[8].

---

[8] Editor's Note: Near Termo lies the Wood-N-Peg Ranch, in the 1970's, a place dedicated to teaching junior high-school girls the ins and outs of western ranching. The girls did everything from clearing brush to caring for horses and goats. Both the editor's daughters spent parts of their junior high summers at the ranch.

Donner Party

The Donner Party was a group of 87 American pioneers who set out in a wagon train headed west for California only to find themselves trapped by snow in the Sierra Nevada. The subsequent casualties resulting from starvation, exposure, disease, and trauma were extremely high, and many of the survivors resorted to cannibalism.

The wagons left Missouri for California in May of 1846. Encouraged to try a new, faster route across Utah and Nevada, they opted to take the Hastings Cutoff proposed by Lansford Hastings, who had never taken the journey with wagons. The Cutoff required the wagons to traverse Utah's Wasatch Mountains and the Great Salt Lake Desert, and slowed the party considerably, leading to the loss of wagons, horses, and cattle. It also forced them to engage in heavy labor by clearing the path ahead of them, and created deep divisions between members of the party. They had planned to be in California by September, but found themselves trapped in the Sierra Nevada by early November.

Most of the party took shelter in three cabins that had been constructed two years earlier at Truckee Lake (now Donner Lake), while a smaller group camped several miles away. Food stores quickly ran out, and a group of 15 men and women attempted to reach California on snowshoes in December, but became disoriented in the mountains before succumbing to starvation and cold. Only seven members of the snowshoe party survived, by eating the flesh of their dead companions. Meanwhile, the Mexican American War delayed rescue attempts from California, although family members and authorities in California tried to reach the stranded pioneers but were turned back by harsh weather.

The first rescue group reached the remaining members, who were starving and feeble, in February 1847. Weather conditions were so bad that three rescue groups were required to lead the rest to California the last arriving in March. Most of these survivors also had resorted to cannibalism. Forty-eight members of the Donner Party survived to live in California. Although a minor incident in the record of westward migration in North America the Donner Party became notorious for the reported claims of cannibalism. Efforts to memorialize the Donner Party were underway within a few years; historians have described the episode as one of the most spectacular tragedies in California history and in the record of western migration.

Donner Lake

Squaw Valley

Olympic Valley (commonly known as Squaw Valley) is an unincorporated community located in Placer County northwest of Tahoe City along Highway 89 on the banks of the Truckee River near Lake Tahoe. It is the home of the Squaw Valley Ski Resort, the site of the 1960 Winter Olympics. It is the smallest place in the world to ever host the Olympic Games.

The 1960 Winter Olympics, officially known as the VIII Olympic Winter Games, were a winter multi-sport event held between 18 and 28 February 1960 in Squaw Valley. Though the 1960 Olympics had practically been promised to Innsbruck, Austria, Cushing went to Paris in 1955 with a scale model of his proposed Olympic site and persuaded the International Olympic Committee to choose Squaw Valley. It was the first Winter Olympics to be televised live and attracted millions of viewers.

Squaw Valley

Squaw Valley was mostly undeveloped, so from 1956 to 1960 all of the venues and infrastructure had to be built or improved at a cost of $80,000,000. The Games featured the first athlete's village and was designed to be intimate, allowing spectators and athletes the ability to walk to nearly all the venues. The opening and closing ceremonies were produced by Walt Disney and televised by CBS. The 1960 Games were the first to have television broadcast rights sold to the highest bidder. It was the first time in 28 years that an Olympic Games had been held in North America.

1960 Winter Olympic Games

Thirty nations and 665 athletes competed in four sports and 27 events. Women's speed skating and biathlon made their Olympic debuts. The organizers decided the bobsled events did not warrant the cost to build a venue, so for the first and only time bobsled was not on the Winter Olympic program. The Soviet Union dominated the medal count winning 21 medals, 7 of which were gold. Soviet speed skaters Yevgeny Grishin and Lidiya Skoblikova were the only multiple gold medalists. Swedish lumberjack Sixten Jernberg added a gold and silver to the 4 medals he won at the 1956 Winter Games. He would win three more in 1964 to finish his Olympic career with 9 medals, becoming the most decorated Winter Olympian to date.

World politics affected the lead-up to the Games with tension between the United States and Soviet Union intensifying, and the International Olympic Committee (IOC) was forced to debate the participation of China, Taiwan, North Korea and East Germany because of the Cold War. In 1957 the United States government threatened to deny visas to athlete from Communist countries, causing the IOC to threaten to revoke Squaw Valley's right to host the 1960 Games. Bowing to international pressure, the United States allowed athletes from Communist countries entry for the Games.

Lake Tahoe

Lake Tahoe is a large freshwater lake in the Sierra Nevada. At a surface elevation of 6,225 ft, it is located along the border between California and Nevada, west of Carson City. Lake Tahoe is the largest alpine lake in North America Its depth is 1,645 ft, making it the USA's second-deepest, the deepest is Crater Lake in Oregon, being 300 ft deeper, at 1,945 ft. Additionally, Lake Tahoe is listed as the 26th largest lake by volume in the world at 122,160,280 acre·ft. Tahoe is also the 16th deepest lake in the world, and the fifth deepest in average depth. It is about 22 mi long and 12 mi wide and has 72 mi of shoreline and a surface area of 191 square miles. Approximately two-thirds of the shoreline is in California.

Lake Tahoe

The lake was formed about 2 million years ago and is a part of the Lake Tahoe Basin with the modern lake being shaped during the ice ages. It is known for the clarity of its water and the panorama of surrounding mountains on all sides. The area surrounding the lake is also referred to as Lake Tahoe, or simply Tahoe.

Vegetation in the basin is dominated by a mixed conifer forest of Jeffrey pine (*Pinus jeffreyi*), lodgepole pine (*P. contorta*), white fir (*Abies concolor*), and red fir (*A. magnifica*). The basin also contains significant areas of wet meadows and riparian areas, dry meadows, brush fields (with *Arctostaphylos* and *Ceanothus*) and rock outcrop areas, especially at higher elevations. *Ceanothus* is capable of fixing nitrogen, but mountain alder (*Alnus tenuifolia*), which grows along many of the basin's streams, springs and seeps, fixes far greater quantities, and contributes measurably to nitrate-N concentrations in some small streams. The beaches of Lake Tahoe are the only known habitat for the rare Lake Tahoe yellowcress (*Rorippa subumbellata*), a plant which grows in the wet sand between low- and high-water marks.

Each autumn, from late September through mid-October, mature kokanee salmon (*Oncorhyncus nerka*), transform from silver-blue color to a fiery vermilion, and run up Taylor Creek, near South Lake Tahoe. As spawning season approaches the fish acquire a humpback and protuberant jaw. After spawning they die and their carcasses provide a feast for gatherings of mink (*Neovison vison*), bears (*Ursus americanus*), and Bald eagles (*Haliaeetus leucocephalus*). These salmon were transplanted from the North Pacific to Lake Tahoe in 1944.

Emerald Bay

Emerald Bay State Park is a California state park, preserving Lake Tahoe's Emerald Bay, a National Natural Landmark. Park features include Eagle Falls and Vikingsholm, a 38-room mansion that is considered one of the finest examples of Scandinavian architecture in the United States. The park contains the only island in Lake Tahoe, Fannette Island. In 1969 Emerald Bay was recognized as a National Natural Landmark by the federal Department of the Interior. In 1994 California State Parks included the surrounding water of the bay as a part of the park, making Emerald

Bay one of the first underwater parks of its type in the state, protecting the various wrecks and other items on the bay's bottom.

Emerald Bay, Lake Tahoe

Section 7

Markleeville to San Ysidro

California 89 to US 395 to California 120 to US 6 to US 395 to California 136 to California 190 to California 127 to Interstate 15 to Interstate 40 to US 95 to Interstate 10 to California 78 to California 111 to California 98 to Interstate 8 to California 94 to California 125 to California 905

Markleeville

Markleeville traces its beginnings to the land claim of Jacob Marklee who established a toll bridge across a tributary of the Carson River in 1861 during the height of the silver mining boom at nearby Silver Mountain City. He recorded his land claim of 160 acres on June 23, 1862, in Douglas County, Nevada, but after the boundary survey, found his claim was in California During the rush to the Comstock Lode, the town of Markleeville was built upon Marklee's land. Marklee hoped to prosper from the freight and supplies headed to the mining camps, but was instead killed in a gunfight in 1863, his killer going free on a plea of self-defense.

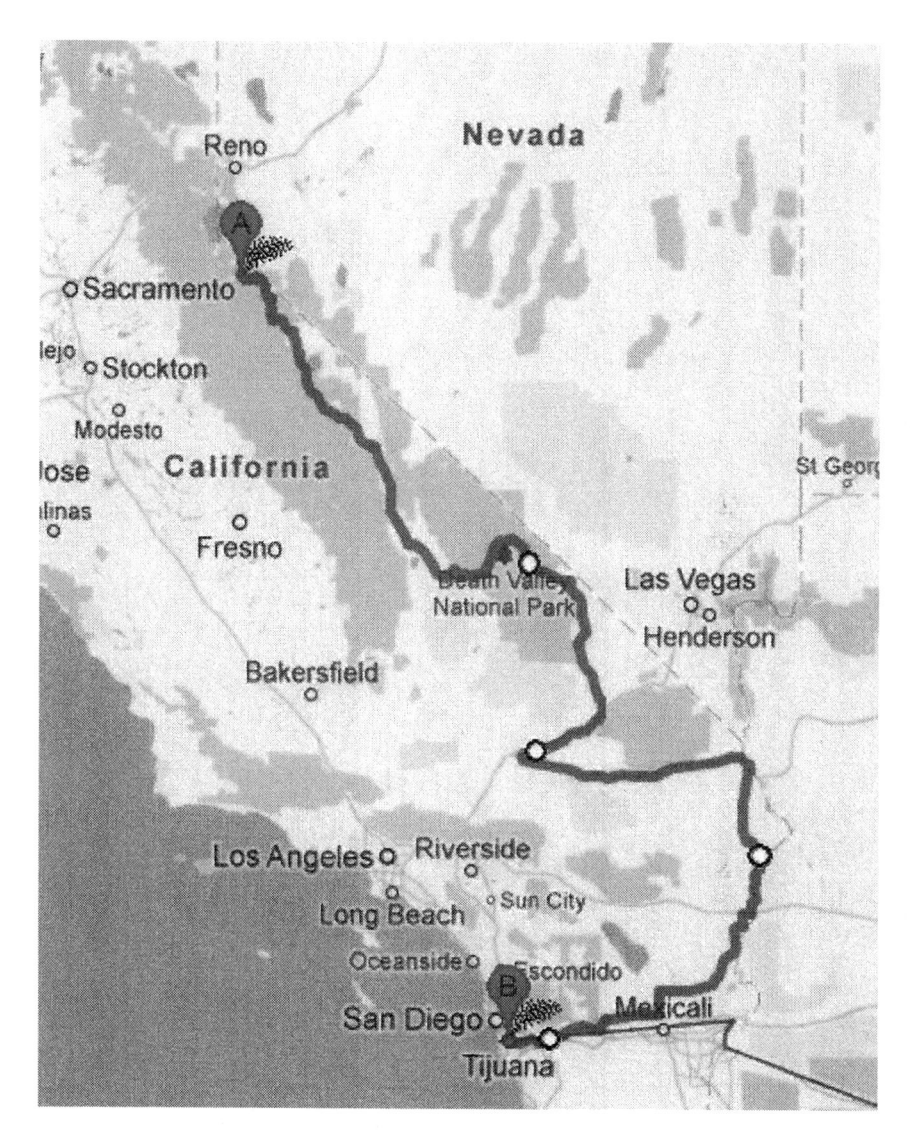

Markleeville to San Ysidro (Google Maps)

Markleeville Courthouse

A post office opened in Markleeville in 1863.

When the mines shut down, Markleeville assumed the county seat and remains the center of government services for Alpine County — the Alpine County Courthouse now occupies the site of Marklee's cabin, which is California Historical Landmark #240. Alpine County is the smallest county, by population, in the state. As of 2010, it had a population of 1,175, all rural.

Snowshoe Thompson: "Viking of the Sierra"

Jill Beede

Sierra Nevada College

When John A. Thompson responded to an ad in the Sacramento Union: "People Lost to the World; Uncle Sam Needs a Mail Carrier", he had no idea he was to become a living legend.

When I cross–country ski under the moonlight through the back country of the Sierra Nevada mountains, I often think of Snowshoe Thompson, one of the most intriguing heroes in California's history. From 1856 to 1876 he made legendary 90 mile treks over snowdrifts up to 50 feet high and through blizzards with up to 80 mile per hour winds, to deliver mail to those living in isolation. He was the sole link between California and the Atlantic states during the long winter months.

Snowshoe Thompson

At the age of 10, Jon Torsteinson–Rue (later changed to John A. Thompson) came to America with his family from Norway, settling on a farm in Illinois. The family moved on to Missouri then Iowa, and eventually Jon went to stay with his brother in Wisconsin. Then gold fever struck.

In 1851 at the age of 24 Thompson drove a herd of milk cows to California and settled in Placerville. For a short while he mined in Kelsey Diggins, Coon Hollow and Georgetown. With the small amount he saved, he bought a small ranch at Putah Creek, in the Sacramento Valley.

All attempts by postmen to cross the Sierra on woven Canadian and Native American snowshoes had failed until one day in late 1855, Thompson saw an ad in the Sacramento Union: "People Lost to the World; Uncle Sam Needs a Mail Carrier." He had had personal experience with mail deprivation, having once received long delayed news of a flu epidemic which claimed his mother's life, and quickly applied for the job.

As a young child in the Telemark region of Norway, ski shaped snow-shoes (called ski–skates) were as common as ordinary shoes. A crowd formed in Placerville for his first mail run in January, 1856. Few had faith that he would make it over the 7,500 foot passes on his homemade 10 foot long, 25 pound oak skis. But one optimistic voice in the crowd called out: "Good luck, Snowshoe Thompson" and he set out to become a legendary postman and father of California skiing.

Two to four times a month for twenty winters, regardless of weather, Snowshoe Thompson set out at the appointed hour. His mail run took 3 days from Placerville to Mormon Station, Utah (Nevada's first town, later called Genoa when Nevada became a state), and two days on the return trip. The people of the pioneer settlement knew when to expect his arrival. Baking was left in the oven and abandoned meals grew cold. Everyone ran outdoors looking up to the top of Genoa Peak to watch as the tall blond norseman descended, streaks of snow flying in his wake.

Thompson always wore a Mackinaw jacket, a wide rimmed hat, and covered his face in charcoal to prevent snow blindness. He carried no blankets, but he did carry matches to start fires, and his bible. He snacked on dried sausage, jerked beef, crackers, and biscuits. When a storm kept him from proceeding he would find a flat rock, clear it of snow, and dance old Norwegian folk dances until it passed, then he would continue on his way. He rested but briefly, and usually only long enough for a crust to form back over the fresh snow, for easier passage.

Dan de Quille of the Virigina City Territorial Enterprise later wrote of Thompson: "He flew down the mountainside. He did not ride astride his pole or drag it to one side as was the practice of other snow–shoers, but held it horizontally before him after the manner of a tightrope walker. His appearance was graceful, swaying his balance pole to one side and the other in the manner that a soaring eagle dips its wings."

Grizzly bears, mountain lions and wolves roamed his path, but he carried no gun, not wanting to limit the weight of mail and much needed supplies. On one trip he came upon a pack of wolves feeding on a deer carcass. When they noticed him, they sat on their haunches and howled. Snowshoe kept his pace, expecting them to attack at any moment, and flew right by them. When he looked back, they had returned to their meal.

Much as his Viking ancestors had traveled upon unmarked waters, Snowshoe Thompson crossed the Sierra Mountains, whose landmarks were buried in the snow. He didn't use a compass, once stating in an interview : "There is no danger of getting lost in a narrow range of mountains like the Sierra, if a man has his wits about him." He could tell his direction by day, from the appearance of trees and rocks, the flow of the streams, animal tracks, and snowdrifts. By night, the formation of stars guided him.

Snowshoe Thompson often rescued prospectors caught in the snow, and would carry them out on the back of his skis as they held their arms around him. One well-known incident took place just before Christmas in 1856, when he found a trapper named James Sisson, who had been sheltering with half-frozen feet in a deserted cabin for 12 days, with no food or fire. Thompson chopped him some wood to stay warm and set out to Genoa for help. He had to carve skis and give lessons to the rescuers who had agreed to accompany him. Once back in Genoa, the doctor reported that Sisson's feet needed to be amputated, but he had no chloroform. Thompson set out once again to Placerville, but there was none to be found, so he continued on to Sacramento. In all he traveled 400 miles in 10 days, and saved Sisson's life.

Sierra Nevada Winter

    His mail sack often weighed up to 100 pounds: carrying medicine, emergency supplies, clothing, books, tools, pots and pans. Once he brought in a pack of needles and a glass chimney for a kerosene lamp so a widow, Mrs. Franklin, could continue her winter sewing. For the local fiddler, Richard Cosser, he brought new strings. And for the news starved miners, he carried the type and newsprint for Nevada's first newspaper, the Territorial Enterprise, piece by piece. The first issue went to press December 18, 1858.

    In 1859 Thompson was asked to take a strange blue rock, which seemed to be devaluing the Washoe miners' gold dust, to Sacramento to have it assayed – it was rich in silver. The Comstock Lode had now been discovered, signaling an end to the California Gold Rush and the glorious 49er era. A new stampede began, this time from west to east and Thompson was asked to expand his mail route to Virginia City, year round.

    As legends of Snowshoe Thompson's feats spread through the isolated regions of the Sierra, others began making skis and racing down the hills. For a short time, during the building of the Central Pacific Railroad, he carried the mail from Cisco to Meadow Lake. During the winter of 1867–68, one of the most severe in history, 3,000 people were met with an unexpected storm and ended up wintering in at Meadow Lake City. Clarence M. Wooster wrote in a letter that Thompson would "sail down his four–mile course at great speed, cross the ice frozen river, throw our mail toward the house, and glide out of sight, up and over a hill, by the momentum gathered in the three mile descent."

Wooster further explained in his letter how he and some kids once gave into their temptation of turning Snowshoe's frozen tracks into a sled run. They shot down the mountain like rockets: "The skis held to the track, but three of the kids went tumbling down a steep mountain." When Thompson heard of the incident he searched out the kids and gave them a spanking they never forgot!

There are a variety of stories of how and when Thompson met his wife, the English woman, Agnes Singleton, who had come to America with her step–mother. My personal favorite is that he gave her ski lessons. They were married in 1866, however there are as many discrepancies as to the location. They settled on the property Thompson had homesteaded a few years earlier in Diamond Valley (Alpine County) – just east and at the foot of the Sierra Nevada mountains, 5 miles to the west of Carson Valley.

Deeply involved in the land and its uses, Thompson raised grains wheat, oats, hay and potatoes. As he explained in letters to his family, the only fruits he could grow were gooseberries and currents, due to the late spring and early fall frosts. He constructed irrigation ditches, from the West Fork of the Carson River to his ranch, that are still in service today. In the winter he cared for 90 head of cattle and 20 horses – half his own, and the rest were boarded for others who lived higher up in the mountains.

The Thompson's only child, Arthur Thomas, was born on February 11, 1867. His father could hardly wait to take him snowshoeing, and made him a tiny pair of snowshoes for his first birthday. In Alpine County, Thompson enjoyed teaching his neighbors how to make snowshoes, giving them lessons and offering chilling demonstrations of his jumps at the top of Silver Mountain. Just as it seemed he was going to run into the onlookers midway down the slope, he would spring up again, flying right over them with a wide smile on his face. In one of his races, he skied 1600 feet in 21 seconds (55 miles per hour), and his greatest jump was known to be 180 feet, in the early 1870s!

From 1868 to 1872 Thompson served on the Board of Supervisors of Alpine County, and was a delegate to the Republican State Convention in Sacramento in 1871. In spite of a resolution sent to Washington, D.C. by the Nevada Legislature, the many political contacts he had gathered, and a trip to Washington, D.C. in 1872, Snowshoe Thompson was never paid for his services delivering the United States Mail.

Snowshoe Thompson died of appendicitis which developed into pneumonia on May 15, 1876. His son, Arthur, died two years later of diphtheria, and was buried next to his father at the cemetery in Genoa. Agnes remarried in 1884, but the following year had a snow–white marble erected on Snowshoe's grave, engraved with a pair of crossed skis and the memento "Gone but not forgotten."

The Genoa postmaster S.A.Kinsey said: "Most remarkable man I ever knew, that Snowshoe Thompson. He must be made of iron. Besides, he never thinks of himself, but he'd give his last breath for anyone else – even a total stranger." The few times Thompson had thought of putting an end to his legendary Snowshoe Express, he continued just for the look on the faces of the people living in isolation. Hundreds of thousands from all parts of the globe emigrated to California in search of gold, but few left such a heartfelt mark on the Golden State's history as John A. "Snowshoe" Thompson.

Death Ride

Located in the stunning California Alps, the Death Ride® course covers the traditional five mountain passes. This super challenging course includes climbing both sides of Monitor Pass, both sides of Ebbetts Pass, and the final climb up the east side of Carson Pass. Cyclists will register and finish at Turtle Rock Park, located two miles north of Markleeville, CA.

Riding 129 miles and climbing 15,000+ feet all in one day is a daunting task! To make this event even more difficult, the course is located in the Sierra Nevada mountains at elevations between 5,000 feet and 8,732 feet.

Death Ride

Mono Lake

Mono Lake (/ˈmoʊnoʊ/ *MOH-noh*) is a large, shallow saline lake in Mono County, formed at least 760,000 years ago as a terminal lake in a basin that has no outlet to the ocean. The lack of an outlet causes high levels of salts to accumulate in the lake. These salts also make the lake water alkaline.

Mono Lake

This desert lake has an unusually productive ecosystem based on brine shrimp that thrive in its waters, and provides critical nesting habitat for two million annual migratory birds that feed on the shrimp. Mono Lake is also notable for containing GFAJ-1, a rod-shaped extremophilic species of bacteria that may be capable of metabolizing the usually poisonous element arsenic.

Mono Lake is believed to have formed at least 760,000 years ago, dating back to the Long Valley eruption. Sediments located below the ash layer hint that Mono Lake could be a remnant of a larger and older lake that once covered a large part of Nevada and Utah, which would put it among the oldest lakes in North America. At its height during the most recent ice age, the lake may have been 900 feet deep. Prominent old shore lines, called strandlines by geologists, can be seen above Lee Vining and along volcanic hills northeast of the current lake.

Currently, Mono Lake is in a geologically active area at the north end of the Mono–Inyo Craters volcanic chain and is close to Long Valley Caldera. Volcanic activity continues in the Mono Lake vicinity: the most recent eruption occurred 350 years ago, resulting in the formation of Paoha Island. Panum Crater (on the south shore of the lake) is an excellent example of a combined rhyolite dome and cinder cone.

On December 2, 2010, NASA announced the discovery of an organism in Mono Lake, named GFAJ-1, that utilizes arsenic in its cellular structure. If confirmed, this would constitute the first discovery of a life form capable of replacing one of the six essential elements (carbon, hydrogen, oxygen, nitrogen, sulfur and phosphorus) in its biomolecules.

U.S. Route 6

U.S. Route 6 (US 6), also called the Grand Army of the Republic Highway, a name that honors an American Civil War veterans association, is a main route of the U.S. Highway system, running east-northeast from Bishop, to Provincetown, Massachusetts. Until 1964, it continued south from Bishop to Long Beach, and was a transcontinental route. After U.S. Route 20, it is the second-longest U.S. highway in the United States and the longest continuous highway.

US Route 6

Prior to a 1964 highway renumbering project, US 6 extended to Long Beach along what is now US 395, California 14, Interstate 5, Interstate 110/California 110, and California 1. Despite the renumbering having removed all freeway portions, it is still part of the California Freeway and Expressway System. US 6's former routing included a short segment of the famous Arroyo Seco Parkway. Currently, US 6 begins at US 395 in Bishop and heads north between farms and ranches in the Chalfant Valley at the base of the 14,000' ft western escarpment of the White Mountains. After about 30 miles Benton is reached, which has a cafe and gas station.

Ancient Bristlecone Pine Forest

The Ancient Bristlecone Pine Forest is high in the White Mountains in Inyo County. The Great Basin Bristlecone Pine (*Pinus longaeva*) trees grow between 9,800 and 11,000 feet above sea level, in xeric alpine conditions, protected within the Inyo National Forest.

The Methuselah Grove in the Ancient Bristlecone Pine Forest is the location of the "Methuselah", a Great Basin Bristlecone Pine more than 4,750 years old. This is 1,000 years older than any other tree in the world. "Methuselah" is not marked in the forest, to ensure added protection from vandals.

Methuselah

Owens Valley

Owens Valley is the arid valley of the Owens River, to the east of the Sierra Nevada and west of the White Mountains and Inyo Mountains on the west edge of the Great Basin section. The mountain peaks on either side (including Mount Whitney) reach above 14,000 feet in elevation, while the floor of the Owens Valley is at 4,000 feet, making the valley one of the deepest in the United States. The Sierra Nevada casts the valley in a rain shadow, which makes Owens Valley "the Land of Little Rain." The bed of Owens Lake, now a predominantly dry endorheic alkali flat, sits on the southern end of the valley.

Owens Valley

In the early 20th century, the valley became the scene of a struggle between local residents and the city of Los Angeles over water rights. William Mulholland, superintendent of the Los Angeles Department of Water and Power (LADWP) planned the 223 miles Los Angeles Aqueduct, completed in 1913, which diverted water from the Owens River. Much of the water rights were acquired through subterfuge, with purchases splitting water cooperatives and pitting neighbors against each other. The purchases led to anger among local farmers, which erupted in violence in 1924, when parts of the water system were sabotaged by local farmers.

Eventually Los Angeles acquired a large fraction of the water rights to over 300,000 acres of land in the valley such that inflows to Owens Lake were almost completely diverted. This acquisition was made following negotiations in which Los

Angeles and the Owens Valley farmers were engaged in a bilateral monopoly. By modern estimates, Los Angeles would have been willing to pay up to $8.70 per acre-foot of water. Eventually the average actual transaction price was near $4.00 per acre-foot, as the next best option was continuing to use the land for agricultural uses, which fetched a much lower price. Although this price was lower than Los Angeles' willingness to pay, the farmers of Owens Valley received a premium for their land compared to land values in neighboring counties. Also, the farmers who were steadfast the longest during the Owens Valley Transfers were able to sell their land for even higher prices than the average farmer received due to Los Angeles' willingness to settle. As a result of these acquisitions, the lake subsequently dried up completely, leaving the present alkali flat which plagues the southern valley with alkali dust storms.

Owens Valley Aquaduct

In 1970, LADWP completed a second aqueduct from Owens Valley. More surface water was diverted and groundwater was pumped to feed the aqueduct. Owens

Valley springs and seeps dried and disappeared, and groundwater-dependent vegetation began to die.

Years of litigation followed. In 1997, Inyo County, Los Angeles, the Owens Valley Committee, the Sierra Club, and other concerned parties signed a Memorandum of Understanding that specified terms by which the lower Owens River would be rewatered by June 2003. LADWP missed this deadline and was sued again. Under another settlement, this time including the state of California, Los Angeles promised to rewater the lower Owens River by September 2005. As of February 2005, LADWP announced it was unlikely to meet this extended deadline. Finally, in 2008, Los Angeles fulfilled its promise and rewatered the lower Owens River.

Mount Whitney

Mount Whitney is the highest summit in the contiguous United States with an elevation of 14,505 feet. It is on the boundary between Inyo and Tulare counties, 84.6 miles west-northwest of the lowest point in North America at Badwater in Death Valley National Park at 282 ft below sea level. The west slope of the mountain is in Sequoia National Park and the summit is the south end of the John Muir Trail which runs 211.9 mi from Happy Isles in Yosemite Valley. The east slope is in the Inyo National Forest in Inyo County.

The summit of Whitney is on the Sierra Crest and near many of the highest peaks of the Sierra Nevada. The peak rises 10,778 ft or just over two miles above the town of Lone Pine in the Owens Valley below.

Mt. Whitney

The eastern slope of Whitney is far steeper than its western slope. This is because the entire Sierra Nevada is the result of a fault-block that is analogous to a door: the door is hinged on the west and is slowly rising on the east. The rise is caused by a normal fault system that runs along the eastern base of the Sierra, below Mount Whitney. Thus, the granite that forms Mount Whitney is the same as the granite that forms the Alabama Hills thousands of feet below. The raising of Whitney (and the downdrop of the Owens Valley) is due to the same geological forces that cause the Basin and Range Province: the crust of much of the intermontane west is slowly being stretched.

The granite that forms Mount Whitney is part of the Sierra Nevada batholith. In Cretaceous time, masses of molten rock that originated from subduction rose underneath what is now Whitney and solidified underground to form large expanses of granite. In the last few million years, the Sierra has started to rise. This has enabled glacial and river erosion to strip the upper layers of rock to reveal the resistant granite that makes up Mount Whitney today.

Mt. Whitney

The most popular route to the summit is by way of the Mount Whitney Trail which starts at Whitney Portal, at an elevation of 8,360 ft, west of the town of Lone Pine. The hike is about 22 mi round trip with an elevation gain of over 6,100 ft. Permits are required year round, and to prevent overuse a limited number of permits are issued by the Forest Service between May 1 and November 1. Most hikers do the trip in two days. Those in good physical condition sometimes attempt to reach the summit and return to Whitney Portal in one day, thus requiring only a somewhat easier-to-obtain "day use" permit rather than the overnight permit. This is considered an "extreme" day hike, which normally involves leaving Whitney Portal before sunrise and 12 to 18 hours of strenuous hiking, while struggling with altitude sickness, cold air, and occasionally treacherous surface conditions (because snow and/or ice are normally present on parts of the trail, except for a short period from early July to late September.)

Longer approaches to Whitney arrive at its west side, connecting to the Mount Whitney Trail near the summit by way of the John Muir Trail.

Death Valley

Death Valley is a desert valley located in Eastern California. Situated within the Mojave Desert, it features the lowest, driest, and hottest locations in North America. Badwater, a basin located in Death Valley, is the specific location (36° 15' N 116° 49.5' W) of the lowest elevation in North America at 282 feet below sea level. This point is only 84.6 miles ESE of Mount Whitney, the highest point in the contiguous United States. Death Valley holds the record for the highest reliably reported temperature in the Western hemisphere, 134 °F at Furnace Creek on July 10, 1913, just short of the world record, 136 °F in 'Aziziya, Libya, on September 13, 1922.

Located near the border of California and Nevada, in the Great Basin, east of the Sierra Nevada mountains, Death Valley constitutes much of Death Valley National Park and is the principal feature of the Mojave and Colorado Deserts Biosphere Reserve. It is located mostly in Inyo County. It runs from north to south between the Amargosa Range on the east and the Panamint Range on the west; the Sylvania Mountains and the Owlshead Mountains form its northern and southern boundaries, respectively. It has an area of about 3,000 sq mi.

Death Valley is one of the best geological examples of a basin and range configuration. It lies at the southern end of a geological trough known as Walker Lane, which runs north into Oregon. The valley is bisected by a right lateral strike slip fault system, represented by the Death Valley Fault and the Furnace Creek Fault. The eastern end of the left lateral Garlock Fault intersects the Death Valley Fault. Furnace Creek and the Amargosa River flow through the valley but eventually disappear into the sands of the valley floor.

The depth and shape of Death Valley influence its summer temperatures. The valley is a long, narrow basin is walled by high, steep mountain ranges. The clear, dry air and sparse plant cover allow sunlight to heat the desert surface. Summer nights provide little relief as overnight lows may only dip into the 82 to 98 °F range. Moving masses of super-heated air blow through the valley creating extreme high temperatures.

Badwater Basin, Death Valley

Death Valley also contains salt pans. According to current geological consensus, during the middle of the Pleistocene era there was a succession of inland seas (collectively referred to as Lake Manly) located where Death Valley is today. As the area turned to desert the water evaporated, leaving behind the abundance of evaporitic salts such as common sodium salts and borax, which were subsequently exploited during the modern history of the region, primarily 1883 to 1907.

Death Valley

The hottest air temperature ever recorded in Death Valley (Furnace Creek) was 134 °F on July 10, 1913, at Furnace Creek, which is currently the hottest temperature ever recorded in the western hemisphere. This record is the highest temperature in July anywhere on the globe. During the heat wave that peaked with that record, five consecutive days reached 129 °F or above. The temperature of 134 °F at Furnace Creek was measured only 3.5 feet off the ground, and is not considered reliable by Christopher Burt. If temperatures are measured at least 4 feet off the ground, as recommended by NOAA, , then the highest temperature in the world would be 129°F at Furnace Creek on July 20, 1960, July 18, 1998, July 20, 2005, July 7, 2007.

Death Valley National Monument was proclaimed on February 11, 1933 by President Hoover, placing the area under federal protection. In 1994, the monument was redesignated as Death Valley National Park, as well as being substantially expanded to include Saline and Eureka Valleys.

Death Valley Race Track

Scotty's Castle

Scotty's Castle is a two-story Mission Revival and Spanish Colonial Revival style villa located in the Grapevine Mountains of northern Death Valley in Death Valley National Park. Scotty's Castle is not a real castle, and it did not belong to the "Scotty" from whom it got its name.

Construction began on Scotty's Castle in 1922, and cost between $1.5 and $2.5 million. A man named Walter Scott born in Cynthiana, Kentucky, also known as "Death Valley Scotty", convinced Chicago millionaire Albert Johnson to invest in his gold mine in the Death Valley area. By 1937, Johnson had acquired more than 1,500 acres in Grapevine Canyon, where the ranch is located.

Scotty's Castle

After Johnson and his wife made several trips to the region, and his health improved, construction began. It was Mrs. Johnson's idea to build something comfortable for their vacations in the area, and the villa eventually became a winter home.

Unknown to the Johnsons, the initial survey was incorrect, and the land they built Death Valley Ranch on was actually government land; their land was further up Grapevine Canyon. Construction halted as they resolved this mistake, but before it could resume, the stock market crashed in 1929, making it difficult for Johnson to finish construction. Having lost a considerable amount of money, the Johnsons used the Death Valley Ranch to produce income by letting rooms out.

Mohave Desert

The Mojave Desert occupies a significant portion of southeastern California and smaller parts of central California, southern Nevada, southwestern Utah and northwestern Arizona. Named after the Mohave tribe of Native Americans, it displays typical basin and range topography.

The Mojave Desert's boundaries are generally defined by the presence of *Yucca brevifolia* (Joshua trees); considered an indicator species for this desert. The topographical boundaries include the Tehachapi together with the San Gabriel and San Bernardino mountain ranges. The mountain boundaries are quite distinct since they are outlined by the two largest faults in California the San Andreas and the Garlock. The Great Basin shrub steppe lies to the north; the warmer Sonoran Desert (the Low Desert) lies to the south and east. The desert is believed to support between 1,750 and 2,000 species of plants.

Joshua Tree, Mojave Desert

The Mojave Desert is defined by the mountain ranges creating its xeric conditions, and it also has numerous mountain ranges within it. They often create valleys, endorheic basins, salt pans, and seasonal saline lakes when precipitation is high enough. These mountain ranges and valleys are part of the Basin and Range province and the Great Basin, a geologic area of crustal thining which pulls open valleys over millions of years. Most of the valleys are internally drained, so all precipitation that falls within the valley does not eventually flow to the ocean. Some of the Mojave (toward the east, in and around the Colorado River/Virgin River Gorge) is within a different geographic domain, the Colorado Plateau. This area is known for its incised canyons, high mesas and plateaus, and flat strata, a unique geographic locality found nowhere else on earth.

Jedediah Smith

Mountain Man ... Desert Man

Bob Katz

University of Californiaat Santa Cruz

Jedediah Smith is probably the most famous of all "Mountain Men" -- those fur-clad, grizzled individuals who were first to explore the American West in search of pelts and adventure. He was the first American (after the Astorians) to cross west over the Continental Divide, rediscovering South Pass, and the first American to traverse California's rugged Sierra Nevada Mountains. He was also first to open the coastal trade route from California to Fort Vancouver on the Columbia River.

But few realized that among his greatest exploits were Jedediah Smith's trail-blazing expeditions across the deserts of the American West. In fact, Jedediah was the first American to enter California overland from the east (across the forbidding Mojave Desert) and the first to cross the enormous Great Basin Desert and return east, overland from California.

Origins

Jedediah Smith was born June 24, 1798, at Bainbridge, New York. While still in his teens, Jedediah joined a fur-trading expedition to the Rocky Mountains, becoming one of the original "Ashley Men," trappers under the command of William Ashley. He continued in the Rocky Mountain fur trade for more than a decade.

Jedediah and his party of trappers spent the winter of 1823-24 with a band of Crow Indians who told him how to reach Utah's Green River. In mid-March 1824, his company rediscovered the South Pass -- a passage to the Northwest through present-day Wyoming -- and descended into the Green River area for the spring hunt.

Explorations

In July 1825, Jedediah attended the first Mountain Man Rendezvous at Henry's Fork then accompanied William Ashley back to St. Louis with the season's bounty of furs. En route downriver, Ashley took Jedediah as partner to replace the retiring Andrew Henry.

In the spring of 1826, Jedediah went ahead of the company's westbound pack train to arrange for that year's Mountain Man Rendezvous, to be held in Cache Valley. That August, he led 17 men to appraise the trapping potential of the region south and west of the Great Salt Lake.

Jedediah Smith

This expedition took him along the route of present-day Interstate 15, the entire length of Utah, to the Virgin River and its eventual confluence with the Colorado River. He followed the Colorado south to the villages of Mojave Indians, then turned his band westward across the Mojave Desert. When he and his band arrived at San Gabriel Mission near present-day Los Angeles, they became the first Americans to cross overland to California entering from the east.

Blocked by the suspicious Mexican governor of California Jedediah changed his plans to explore Oregon and journeyed to the American River near Sacramento instead. In the spring of 1827, he left his party on the Stanislaus River, and taking two trappers, traversed the Sierra Nevada Mountains over Border Ruffian Pass. He then crossed the Great Basin Desert through Nevada, roughly following the route of present-day US Highway 6.

His band reached the Utah-Nevada border near present Grandy, Utah, continued on to Skull Valley and reached the south tip of the Great Salt Lake two days later. By the time they arrived at the 1827 Mountain Man Rendezvous at present-day Laketown, they had become the first Americans to return from California by an overland route.

Later in 1827 Jedediah, with 18 men, retraced his steps from Great Salt Lake to southern California But this time, Mojave Indians attacked his party while crossing the Colorado River, killing 10 men and capturing all the horses. The remainder made their way to California and into the clutches of Mexican officials waiting to incarcerate them.

Legal issues finally resolved, his band spent the winter of 1827-28 in the San Francisco Bay area. In the spring of 1828, after traveling north up the coast to Oregon, their encampment was attacked by Kelawatset Indians near Smith's Fork on the Umpqua River. The four survivors of the attack, including Smith, finally reached Canada's Fort Vancouver in mid-August 1828, where they spent the following winter.

In March of 1829, Jedediah journeyed east, arriving in August at Pierre's Hole, site of that year's Mountain Man Rendezvous. At the following year's 1830 Rendezvous on the Wind River, Jedediah and his two partners sold their trapping interests to the Rocky Mountain Fur Company and became involved in the Santa Fe fur trade.

On May 27, 1831, while en route to Santa Fe, Jedediah Smith was surrounded and killed by Comanche Indians at a water hole near the Cimarron River. His body was never found.

Legacy

Jedediah Smith's pioneering memory is honored in a number of ways including:

- A Birthday Celebration for Jedediah Smith is held in January at the Stockton, California Wildlife Museum. The 200th Birthyear Celebration for relatives of Jedediah Smith was celebrated in 1999.

- The Jedediah Smith Society holds two regular membership meetings per year, one in April at the time of the California History Institute at UOP, and a fall "rendezvous" in late September or early October at a historic location on or near one of Jed Smith's known campsites.

A number of locations in the U.S. also celebrate Smith's legacy:

- The Jedediah Smith Wilderness includes most of the western slope of Wyoming's famous Teton Range.
- The Jediedah Smith Redwood State Park near Crescent City, California offers camping and outdoor activities.
- The Smith River in California includes 46 tributaries that are protected.
- Smith River National Recreation Area in northern California offers camping and outdoor activities.
- The Jedediah Smith Memorial Bicycle Trail runs along 32 miles of parkway from Old Sacramento, California to Folsom Lake.
- Jedediah Smith Society: History Department, University of the Pacific, Stockton, CA 95211.

World's Tallest Thermometer

The world's tallest thermometer is a landmark located in Baker. It is technically an electric sign rather than a tall thermometer. However, it exists as a tribute to the record 134 degrees Fahrenheit recorded in nearby Death Valley on July 10, 1913. Weighing in at 76,812 pounds and held together by 125 cubic yards of concrete, its temperature readings may be viewed from three different angles. It stands 134 feet tall and is capable of displaying a maximum temperature of 134, both of which are a reference to the temperature record.

World's Tallest Thermometer

Colorado River

    The Colorado delineates the entirety of the Arizona–California border, and is impounded by a series of dams, including Imperial Dam, where most of its flow is diverted into the All-American Canal to irrigate the Imperial Valley. Below the confluence with the Gila River the Colorado forms a short stretch of the Mexico–United States border before passing entirely into Mexico.

Colorado River

Prior to channelization of the lower Colorado in the 20th century, the river was characterized by sweeping meanders, sandbars and islands that were subject to frequent course changes. Joseph C. Ives, who surveyed the lower river in 1861, wrote that "the shifting of the channel, the banks, the islands, the bars is so continual and rapid that a detailed description, derived from the experiences of one trip, would be found incorrect, not only during the subsequent year, but perhaps in the course of a week, or even a day."

In 1900, entrepreneurs of the California Development Company (CDC) looked to the Imperial Valley of Southern California as an excellent location to develop agriculture irrigated by the waters of the river. Engineer George Chaffey was hired to design the Alamo Canal, which split off from the Colorado River near Pilot Knob, curved south into Mexico, and dumped into the Alamo River, a dry arroyo which had historically been observed to carry flood flows of the Colorado into the Salton Sink. With a stable year-round flow in the Alamo River, irrigators in the Imperial Valley were able to begin large-scale farming and small towns in the region started to expand with the influx of job-seeking migrants. By 1903, more than

100,000 acres in the valley were under cultivation, supporting a growing population of four thousand.

Alamo River

It was not long before the Colorado River began to wreak havoc with its erratic flows. In autumn, the river would drop below the level of the canal inlet and temporary brush diversion dams had to be constructed. In early 1905, heavy floods destroyed the headworks of the canal and water began to flow uncontrolled down the canal towards the Salton Sink. On August 9, the entire flow of the Colorado swerved into the canal and began to flood the bottom of the Imperial Valley. In a desperate gamble to close the breach, crews of the Southern Pacific Railroad, whose tracks ran through the valley, attempted to dam the Colorado above the canal only to see their work demolished by a flash flood. It took seven attempts, over US$3 million and two years for the railroad, the CDC and the federal government to permanently block the breach and send the Colorado on its natural course back to the gulf – but not before part of the Imperial Valley was flooded under a 45-mile-long lake, today's Salton Sea.

Plank Road

The Old Plank Road is a plank road in Imperial County, that was built in 1915 as an east–west route over the Algodones Dunes. It effectively connected the extreme lower section of Southern California to Arizona and provided the last link in a commercial route between San Diego and Yuma.

Old Plank Road

Following Los Angeles' winning the right to be the western terminus of the transcontinental railroad, San Diego's civic leaders proposed the Plank Road to ensure their city became the hub of Southern California's road network rather than Los Angeles.

Among those promoters was businessman and road builder "Colonel" Ed Fletcher who accepted a challenge from the *Los Angeles Examiner* to run a road race in October 1912 to determine the best route between Southern California and Phoenix. A reporter with the paper was given a 24-hour head start in Los Angeles; Fletcher would proceed from San Diego. Fletcher elected to traverse the constantly shifting sand dunes using a team of horses to pull his automobile through the sand, and won the race in a seemingly impossible 19.5 hours.

Buoyed by the success of the race and with the backing of local newspapers, Fletcher raised the money to pay for 13,000 planks shipped from San Diego to Holtville. The first planks were laid on February 14, 1915 with the help of both volunteers and paid labor. The roadbed consisted of two parallel plank tracks, each 25 inches wide, spiked to wooden crosspieces laid underneath. Total length of the Plank Road was 6.5 miles. Work ended nearly two months later on April 4.

Though traffic and maintenance crews who cleared the wooden road with mule-drawn scrapers soon took its toll on the planking, the road was considered a success. In June that same year, the California State Highway Commission assumed responsibility for the Plank Road as part of the road system linking Southern California with Arizona.

A second, more sophisticated Plank Road was commissioned in 1916. The new roadway consisted of prefabricated wooden sections laid to a width of 8 feet with double-width turnouts every 1000 feet. The sections were shipped to the work site via horse-drawn wagon from their assembly point in nearby Ogilby, and then lowered into place using a crane.

For the next ten years, work crews struggled against the elements to keep the Plank Road open. The cost and difficulty of the maintenance coupled with improved road technology — not to mention the incredibly rough ride the planks created and the fact that the road was only wide enough for a single vehicle — meant that the days of the Plank Road were numbered.

A new, 20-foot-wide road with an asphaltic concrete surface constructed on top of a built-up sand embankment replaced the Old Plank Road upon its opening on

August 12, 1926. This same roadway would later become displaced by U.S. Route 80, itself since displaced by Interstate 8.

Today, only fragments of the Plank Road remain. They are protected under the jurisdiction of the Bureau of Land Management. Additionally, the fragments are both a California Historical Landmark and eligible for inclusion in the National Register of Historic Places. Remnants of the Plank Road may be seen at the west end of Grays Well Road, a frontage road south of I-8. A monument to the Plank Road and interpretive display lie approximately three miles/5.4 km west of the Sand Hills interchange. The monument's largest feature is a 1500-foot-meter-long replica of the road created in the early 1970s out of existing fragments.

Pacific Southwest Railway Museum

The Pacific Southwest Railway Museum, located at the corner of State Route 94 and Forrest Gate Road near Campo, is a railroad museum dedicated to the preservation and interpretation of railroads as they existed in the Pacific Southwest. The museum operates a heritage railroad that offers train rides (including some to Tecate, Mexico), and has 6 steam locomotives, 12 diesel locomotives and 59 other pieces of rolling stock.

Pacific Southwest Railroad Heritage Excursion

Olympic Training Center, Chula Vista

The U.S. Olympic Training Center in Chula Vista, is the first USOC training center to be master-planned from the ground up and is dedicated to the development and performance of America s future Olympic and Paralympic athletes. The year-round, warm-weather facility was a gift to the United States Olympic Committee from the San Diego National Sports Training Foundation, a group of dedicated business and community leaders and volunteers who raised the funds to build the Center.

Olympic Training Center

The Chula Vista Olympic Training Center rests on a 155-acre complex adjacent to Lower Otay Reservoir in San Diego County. The Center has sport venues and support facilities for archery, beach volleyball, BMX, canoe/kayak, cycling, field hockey, rowing, rugby, soccer, softball, tennis, track & field, triathlon, and cross-training abilities for various winter sports. Athletes are selected to train at the CVOTC by their respective sport federation or National Governing Body (NGB). The CVOTC offers support to athletes including housing, dining, training facilities, local transportation, recreational facilities, athlete services and professional development programs.

The Chula Vista Olympic Training Center, which officially opened in June 1995, has benefited thousands of Olympic hopefuls, numerous community groups, and countless visitors from around the globe.

Surf City, 82
1000 Steps Beach, 66
1925 earthquake, 141, 142, 146
1960 Winter Olympics, 255
30th Space Wing, 155
Alabama Hills, 277
Alamo Canal, 291
Alamo River, 291, 292
Alcatraz, 215, 216
Algodones Dunes, 293
All-American Canal, 290
All-American Road, 64
Alphonse, 113
Alpine County, 262, 267, 268
America, 75
Ancient Bristlecone Pine Forest, 272, 273
Angel Island, 216, 217
Angel's Gate Park, 100
Aquarium of the Pacific, 92
Arcata, 238, 239
Arlington Theater, 142, 143, 144
Army Corps of Engineers, 115, 218
Arnold Schwarzenegger, 121
Association of Jesuit Colleges and Universities, 109
Avenue of the Giants, 232, 233
Badwater, 276, 279, 280
Balboa Fun Zone, 71
Balboa Island, 68, 69, 70, 71
Balboa Island Ferry, 71

Balboa Park, 25, 27, 28, 29, 30, 31, 32, 35, 36, 38, 39, 40, 41
Balboa Pavilion, 69, 70, 71
Balboa Pier, 69, 71, 80
Ballona Creek, 115
Beach Boys, 73, 74, 76, 81
Beck, 78, 79
Bellarmine College of Liberal Arts, 113
Belmont Shore, 87
Big Sur, 64, 78, 170, 171
Bigfoot, 240, 241, 242
Bigfoot Scenic Byway, 242
Bill Shoemaker, 53
Bing Crosby, 52, 53
Bishop Montgomery, 117
Blue Riband, 94
Bob Hope Airport, 103
Bolsa Chica wetlands, 83
Border Field State Park, 12, 13, 15
Botanical Building, 30, 32, 34
Boyz-N-The-Hood, 78
Brothers of St. Patrick, 118, 119
Cable car, 194, 195
Cabrillo Bridge, 27, 29, 34, 39, 40
California, 74
California 1, 9, 62, 77, 78, 87, 104, 137, 153, 185, 272
California Coastal Commission, 229
California Dreamin', 74, 76

California Girls, 74, 76
California Historical Landmark, 16, 262, 295
California Love, 74, 75
California Pacific International Exposition, 25
California playlist, 73
California Sunset, 74
California Surfing Museum, 56
California Western Railroad, 230
Californication, 74
Camp Pendleton, 57, 58, 59
Campo, 295
Cannery Row, 176
Carlsbad Flower Fields, 55
Carly Simon, 79
Carousel, 122, 123
Carson Mansion, 234, 235
Cascade Range, 242, 244, 250
Cascade Volcanic Arc, 244
Chaffee, 97
Chandelier Tree, 233
Channel Islands, 51, 131, 133, 134, 135, 152
Channel Islands National Park, 133
Charles I. D. Looff, 122
Charles S. Howard, 52
Christmas Boat Parade, 70
Chula Vista,, 296
Clam Festival, 158
Claude Thornhill, 79

Coast Redwood, 222
Coast Redwoods, 232
Colorado River, 285, 287, 288, 290, 291, 292
Coronado, 13, 14, 15, 17, 18
Coronado Bay Bridge, 17, 18
Costa Mesa, 78, 80
Cristianitos Fault,, 59
Cunard Line, 93, 94
Custom House, 173, 174
Dana Point, 8, 9, 10, 62, 63, 65
Dana PointHarbor, 65, 66
Danny O'Keefe, 78
Death Ride, 268, 269
Death Valley, 276, 279, 280, 281, 282, 283, 289
Death Valley National Park, 276, 279, 281, 282
Del Mar, 52, 53
Del Mar Racetrack, 52
Devil's Slide, 187, 188
Diamonds On My Windshield, 78
Donner Lake, 253, 254
Donner Party, 253, 254
Dwight D. Eisenhower, 116
Eazy-E,, 78
Eel River, 232, 233
El Fureidis, 139, 140
El Prado, 28, 30
Emerald Bay, 258, 259
Emperor Norton, 196, 197, 201,

202, 204, 205, 210, 211, 212, 214, 215
Estimated Prophet, 74
Exclusion Act, 217
Festival of Arts, 67, 68
Fisherman's Wharf, 174, 175, 176, 194, 200
Fort Bragg, 229, 230, 231
Fort Point, 218, 219
Fort Ross, 224, 225
Freeman, 97
Furnace Creek, 279, 281
Gaston, 113
Gauchos, 148
George Woolf, 52
Getty Villa, 128, 129
Giant Dipper, 179
Glacier, 242, 245, 247
Glenn Miller, 79
Going Back to Cali, 74
Going to California", 74
Golden Gate Bridge, 62, 219, 220, 221
Golden Gate National Recreation Area, 221
Golden Gate Park, 189, 190, 191, 192, 193
Goleta, 146, 149
Good Time Charlie's Got the Blues, 78
Grand Prix, 90, 91
Grapevine Canyon, 282, 283
Grateful Dead, 74
Great Basin, 250, 272, 273, 279, 284, 285, 287
Great Basin Bristlecone Pine, 272, 273
Gripman, 194, 195
Grissom, 97
GROMS, 82
Half Moon Bay, 8, 185, 186
Hang gliding., 177
Harbor Light, 96, 97
Harbor Lights, 79, 80
Harry Culver, 110
Hearst Castle, 162, 163, 164, 165, 166, 167, 168, 169, 170
Highway 101, 62, 137
Hollywood Walk of Fame, 122
Hotel California, 74, 80
Hotel del Coronado, 14, 16
Hughes Aircraft, 112
Humboldt Bay, 236
Humboldt County, 233, 239
Humboldt Redwoods State Park, 232
Huntington Beach, 75, 81, 82, 83, 84, 85
Huntington Beach Oil Field, 84
I Love L.A, 74, 77
Imperial Beach, 13, 14
Imperial County, 14, 293
Imperial County, a, 14
Imperial Valley, 14, 290, 291, 292
Incline railway, 113

Inyo County, 272, 276, 279
Inyo Mountains, 273
J. Paul Getty, 129
Jack LaLanne, 119, 121
James Doolittle, 107
Jan & Dean, 74
Japanese Americans, 247, 248
Jedediah Smith, 285, 286, 287, 288, 289
Jimmy Durante, 52
Joe Beek, 70
John McLaren, 190
John Muir, 222, 223, 276, 278
John Steinbeck, 176
John Wayne Airport, 103
Johnston McCulley, 45
Joni Mitchell,, 74
Joshua Abraham Norton, 197, 198
Joshua trees, 284
Juan Rodriguez Cabrillo, 161
Julia Morgan, 162, 164
Kalmia Lake, 242
Kate Sessions, 28, 34
Kayaking, 239
Korean Bell of Friendship, 100
Kruse Rhododendron State Reserve, 225, 227
Kumeyaay, 50
L.A. Woman, 73, 74
La Monica Ballroom, 123
LA/Ontario International Airport, 103

Laguna Beach, 67, 68, 75, 78
Lake Tahoe, 8, 236, 237, 254, 257, 258, 259
Lava Beds National Monument, 250, 251
Lava tubes, 251
Lavacicles, 251
LAX, 102, 103, 104, 105, 106, 107, 108, 109
Led Zeppelin, 74
Leggett, 62, 233
Life in the Fast Lane, 73, 80
Ligaroti, 52
LL Cool J, 74
Lompoc, 152, 155
Long Beach, 62, 63, 87, 88, 89, 90, 91, 92, 94, 95, 96, 97, 99, 103, 271, 272
Los Alamitos Bay, 87, 89
Los Angeles, 8, 24, 47, 53, 64, 68, 87, 88, 89, 96, 98, 99, 100, 102, 103, 104, 105, 107, 108, 109, 110, 111, 112, 113, 114, 115, 116, 119, 124, 125, 133, 140, 145, 146, 159, 163, 165, 168, 210, 274, 276, 287, 293, 294
Los Angeles County, 87, 88, 114, 115, 116, 124, 125
Los Angeles Harbor, 96, 98
Los Angeles International Airport, 102, 103, 104

Los Angeles Pacific Railway, 113
Low Rider, 79
Loyalty oath's, 248
Loyola Law School, 111
Loyola Marymount University, 109, 110, 111, 112
Mad River, 239, 240
Malibu, 77, 125, 126, 128, 129, 182
Malibu Colony, 127
Malone Student Center, 111
Mamas & the Papas, 74, 76
Marin County, 219, 221
Marina del Rey, 112, 114, 115, 116
Marina Del Rey, 111, 114
Marine Corps, 57, 58, 149
Maritime Museum, 23
Markleeville, 8, 260, 261, 262, 269
Marymount College, 111
Maverick's, 185
Medicine Lake Volcano, 250
Mendocino, 62, 229, 230
Mendocino County, 62, 229, 230
Methuselah, 273
Midway, 21, 22
Mines Field, 104
Mission Bay, 48, 49, 50, 212
Mission Santa Barbara, 144, 145, 146, 160

Mojave Desert, 279, 284, 285, 287
Monarch Butterfly Natural, 183
Mono Lake, 269, 270, 271
Monsignor Nicholas Conneally, 117
Montecito, 139, 140
Monterey, 78, 172, 174, 175, 176, 177, 178
Morro Bay, 161, 162
Morro Rock, 161
Motel Inn of San Luis Obispo, 158, 159
Mount Shasta, 244, 245, 246, 247
Mount Whitney, 273, 276, 277, 278, 279
Msgr. Raymond O'Flagherty, 118
Mudslides, 128
Muir Woods National Monument, 221, 223
Municipal Pier, 122
Muscle Beach., 119
Museum of Contemporary Art, 24
Nancy Reagan, 152
Naples, 87, 88
National Historic Landmark, 16, 25, 39, 162, 170, 179, 215, 224
National Register of Historic

Places, 24, 25, 39, 45, 104, 170, 224, 229, 235, 238, 295
Natural Bridges State Beach, 183, 184
Nature Conservancy, 131, 134
Neil Young, 74
Newport Bay, 68
Newport Beach, 72, 78, 81, 182
Noel Richardson, 52
Ocean Institute, 66
Oceanside, 56, 57, 182
Oil Field, 85
Oil islands, 97
Old Town, 44, 45, 234
Oliver Hardy, 52
Orange County, 62, 68, 73, 79, 81
Owens Valley, 273, 274, 275, 276, 277
Pacific Coast Highway, 62, 126, 127, 128
Pacific Electric Railway, 69
Pacific Southwest Railway Museum, 295
Pacifica, 60, 187
Pageant of the Masters, 67, 68
Palisades Park, 124, 125
Palm Canyon, 54
Panama-California Exposition, 24, 30, 35, 165
Panama–California Exposition, 25

Panama–California Exposition, 33
Pat O'Brien, 52
Patricia Brown, 150, 151
Pebble Beach, 172, 173
Petco Park, 19
PETER LARSEN, 73
Pilgrim, 66
Pismo Beach, 157, 158
Pismo clam, 158
Placer County, 254
Plank road, 293
Playa Del Rey, 111, 113, 114
Playland Arcade, 124
Pleasure Pier, 122
Point Conception, 133, 154
Point Conception Lighthouse, 154
Port of Long Beach, 89, 97
Port of Los Angeles, 89, 99, 109, 115
Pylons, 108
Pythian Castle, 238, 239
Queen Mary, 93, 94, 95, 96, 208
Queen of the Missions, 145
Rainbow Harbor, 92
Rancho del Cielo, 152, 153
Randy Newman, 74, 77
Red Hot Chili Peppers, 74
Rhododendron, 226
Richard Henry Dana, 66
Richard Nixon, 60

Rincon, 137, 199, 200
Robert "Wingnut" Weaver, 180, 181
Robot light, 96
Ronald Reagan, 150, 152, 153
Rotchev House, 224
Roy Ropp, 68
S.C.L.S, 101, 102
Salton Sea, 292
Salton Sink, 291, 292
Samoa, 236, 238
Samoa Cookhouse, 236
San Diego, 9, 10, 12, 13, 14, 15, 16, 17, 18, 19, 21, 22, 23, 24, 25, 26, 27, 28, 32, 33, 50, 51, 52, 53, 54, 57, 58, 59, 78, 165, 183, 293, 294, 296, 297
San Diego Bay, 13, 15, 16, 17, 23
San Diego Botanic Gardens, 53
San Diego Convention Center, 19, 20
San Diego High School, 26, 31
San Diego Padres, 19
San Diego River, 48
San Diego Trolley, 10, 12, 19, 25
San Diego Union Station, 25
San Diego Zoo, 25, 26, 31, 41, 43
San DiegoBay, 16
San DiegoConvention Center, 21
San DiegoZoo, 42, 44
San Francisco, 33, 64, 99, 140, 159, 163, 189, 191, 192, 193, 194, 196, 198, 199, 200, 201, 203, 204, 207, 208, 210, 211, 212, 213, 214, 215, 217, 218, 219, 221, 227, 233, 288
San Francisco Bay, 64, 99, 215, 218, 219, 222, 288
San Onofre Nuclear Generating Station, 59, 60
San Pedro, 96, 98, 99, 100, 109, 115, 133
San Simeon, 162, 163, 164
San Ysidro, 9, 11, 260, 261
San YsidroBorder Crossing, 9
Santa Barbara, 62, 73, 84, 133, 134, 138, 139, 140, 141, 142, 143, 145, 146, 147, 148, 149, 150, 151, 152, 154
Santa Barbara Courthouse, 141, 142
Santa Barbara Polo Club, 138
Santa Barbara., 84
Santa Cruz, 8, 131, 132, 134, 177, 178, 179, 181, 182, 183, 184, 285
Santa Fe Depot, 23, 24
Santa Lucia Range, 163
Santa Monica Mountains, 152
Santa Monica Pier, 119, 122, 123
Santa Rosa Dormitory, 151

Santa Ynez Mountains, 138, 145, 151, 152, 153
Santa Ynez River, 152
Sapphire Lake, 242
sasquatch, 240
Scotia, 233, 234
Scotty's Castle, 282, 283
Sea Ranch, 227, 228
Seabiscuit, 52
Seacliff Beach, 177
Seal Beach, 81, 85, 86
Seal Beach Naval Weapons Station, 85, 86
Sepulveda Boulevard, 104, 108
Shasta River, 245
Shastina, 246
SHREDDER, 82
Sierra Club, 222, 276
Sierra Nevada, 198, 222, 242, 253, 257, 262, 263, 266, 267, 269, 273, 276, 277, 279, 285, 287
Silver Strand, 15, 16
Siskiyou County, 244
Sisters of the Holy Names, 117, 119
Skunk Train, 230, 231
Snowshoe Thompson, 262, 263, 264, 265, 266, 268
Sonoma County, 224, 227
South Laguna Beach, 66
Squaw Valley, 254, 255, 257
SS *Palo Alto*, 177, 178

St. Monica Catholic High School, 117, 118, 119
St. Robert's Hall,, 110
St. Vincent's College, 110
State Route 47, 98
Stearns Wharf, 140, 141
Sublime, 73, 77
Surf City, 73, 74, 81, 82
Surf Dog, 82
Surfin' USA, 74
Tecolote Ranunculus, 55
Temple of Kwan Tai, 229, 230
Terminal Island, 98, 99
Termo, 251, 252
the 'Bu, 125
The Doors, 73, 74
The Eagles,, 74, 80
The O.C., 72
The Pike, 91
The Torrey Pine, 51
Theme Building, 105, 106
Thompson Peak, 242, 243
Tijuana, 9, 12, 13, 14
To Live and Die In L.A, 75
Tom Bradley, 107
Tom Waits, 78
Torrance, 101
Torrey Pines, 51
Torrey Pines State Natural Reserve, 50, 51
Trinity Alps, 242, 243
Trinity Alps Wilderness, 242
Trinity County, 239

Truckee River, 254
Tule Lake Internment Center, 247, 248, 249
Tupac Shakur, 74, 75
U.S. Olympic Training Center, 296
U.S. Route 6, 271
UCSB, 146, 147, 148, 149, 150, 151
University of California Santa Barbara,, 146
Vandenberg Air Force Base, 152, 155, 156
Vasco Núñez de Balboa, 25
Ventura Bus Stop, 135, 136
Ventura Highway, 74, 75
Victorian Architecture, 234
Vikingsholm, 258
Vincent Thomas Bridge, 98, 99
W.S. Collins, 68
Walter Scott, 282
War, 79
Westchester, 103, 104, 110, 113
Western White House, 60, 61, 153
When the Swallows Come Back to Capistrano, 79
Where It's At, 79
White, 97
White Island, 97
White Mountains, 272, 273
Whitney Glacier, 245, 246
Whitney Portal, 278
William Hammond Hall, 189
William Mulholland, 274
William Randolph Hearst, 162, 163, 169
William W. Mines, 104
Wilson Park, 101
Wood-N-Peg Ranch, 252
World War II Valor in the Pacific National Monument, 247, 250
World's tallest thermometer, 289
Xavier Hall, 110
You're So Vain, 79
Yreka, 243, 244
Zorro, 45, 46, 47, 48
Zuma Beach, 127

Other Travel books by Don W. Lake include "On the All American road."

Made in the USA
San Bernardino, CA
17 January 2019